"The Little Book on Relationship *is comforting, yet compelling. After John English overcame addiction and self-doubt, he opened to deeper teachings and traditions, becoming a gentle and confident guide for those who wish to grow more generous in all their relationships. In these few pages he makes three big promises: first how to be honest and loving with yourself, then to mirror the same with others, and finally to open to connection to Spirit. He delivers on all three.*"

— Cynthia L. Wall, LCSW author of
The Courage to Trust: a guide to deep and lasting relationships

"*Don't let this little book fool you* — *it contains simple secrets, hope, and wisdom that will empower you and change your life. A must-read for anyone on the spiritual path.*"

— Joanne Tedesco, editor, *Arizona Networking News*

"*Bravo to John English for another runaway success. The Little Book on Relationship is engaging and embodies a powerful truth. John's approach is fresh and innovative, and reminds us all that life itself is awareness. I highly recommend this book for anyone who has ever dared to dream.*"

— Bronwyn Marmo, award-winning author of
The Food Is a Lie: The Truth Is Within

"*The Little Book on Relationship is a masterpiece! John English takes the reader on a step-by-step journey to the realization and understanding of relationship. This book will benefit those who seek meaning in relationship from an academic as well as a spiritual perspective. It speaks to all and transcends specific viewpoints, philosophies, and traditions. I highly recommend it for all who seek to have a better understanding of functioning in the outer world with others and functioning in the inner world with self!*"

— Marilyn Rossner, Ph.D., Ed.D.,
Vice President, IIIHS, Behavior Therapist,
Yoga Therapist and Instructor

"*John's workshop expanded my perception of how I view relationships. I [am able to] use the concepts I learned not only for my own growth, but also in my work with my clients in healing their relationships with themselves and with others. John has an exceptional gift for explaining difficult concepts in a simple, understandable way [that people can use in their everyday lives].*"

— Barb, client and Medicine Wheel student,
Black Canyon City, Arizona

"*The concepts I learned in John's workshop gave me a new sense of empowerment. [In the past] I had experienced feelings of helplessness and bewilderment about the purpose of relationships. Now I am learning to see, with wonder and awe, the gifts that are hidden in all my relationships.*"

— Leann, client and Medicine Wheel student,
Phoenix, Arizona

Also by John English

THE SHIFT: AN AWAKENING

The Little Book on
Relationship

How to Guide Your Life with Meaning, Purpose and Power

John English

DREAMTIME LLC

The Little Book on Relationship

How to Guide Your Life with Meaning, Purpose and Power

Copyright © 2009 by John English

Dreamtime LLC
4715 E. Lone Cactus Drive
Phoenix, AZ 85050
www.mydreamtimellc.com

Book design: Michael Brechner / Cypress House
Cover design: Elizabeth Petersen / Mendocino Graphics

Publisher's Cataloging-in-Publication Data

English, John, 1962-
  The little book on relationship : universal power in daily life / John English. -- 1st ed. -- Phoenix, Ariz. : Dreamtime Pub., c2009.
    p. ; cm.
  ISBN: 978-0-9727034-6-8
  1. Interpersonal relations. 2. Relationship quality. 3. Spiritual life. I. Title.
  HM1106 .E54 2009   2008943343
  302.1--dc22 0903

PRINTED IN THE UNITED STATES OF AMERICA

2 4 6 8 9 7 5 3

For Laurie, my partner, lover, companion, and best friend

Acknowledgements

I am going to start by acknowledging YOU. Never would I have been inspired into sharing the processes in this book if you had not called me to do so. Of all the people I am going to thank I have to start with you, because it is your life that has the potential to be changed by the reading of this book. If you begin to use the power inherent in relationship, this will impact our world positively beyond what we can imagine. For this I am extremely grateful.

I want to thank all of you who have worked tirelessly and with passion to make this world a better place. This includes all of you who strive to shine your LIGHT on everyone you meet. Please remember that your little actions of the heart add up to huge positive forces for humanity.

Over the last forty years a growing group of people have evolved who can best be described as conscious people. I want to thank each of you for all of the work you have done on yourselves to realize your potential as divine beings and for all you have done to share your lives with others.

So many great people have mentored me throughout the last twenty years in multiple areas of my life. You all know who you are; I thank you and bless you. Particularly I want to thank Kent Silberman for mentoring me in the way of the shaman and Alberto Villoldo for my initiation into the Q'ero lineage. Thank you, Th'eun Mares, for your volumes on the Toltec teachings. I want to thank all of our teachers—those who have come forward at this time to write and teach, as well as the teachers we meet every day as we experience the great gift and game of life.

I want to acknowledge all of my students for their support and dedication to my work at Dreamtime, LLC and mostly for their dedication to living their full potential in this lifetime with an eye on making this world a better place. I extend a big heart-felt "thank you" to the Dream Team—the Dreamtime staff, both past and present.

Stacey Badger and Suzy Jimerson-Overholt, thank you for your vision, patience and dedication in *seeing* this project through with your editing skills. Thank you,

Acknowledgements

Keylaira Lee, for your artwork of the sun symbol.

We all owe a great debt of gratitude to all of the indigenous cultures across the globe that have been sharing their ancient wisdom and approaches to life. Words cannot express how thankful I am for these acts. Despite everything that has happened, you chose to remind us about walking in beauty.

Lastly, I want to thank my children for choosing me as their father. I love them so much and they have been my greatest teachers. Thank you, Patrick, Kailee and Melissa. To my dear wife, Laurie—you still light up my life, and from the bottom of my heart I thank you for your support and encouragement to fulfill my potential and be a light in this world.

Contents

Introduction

In this little book you will learn about using the *power of relationship* to navigate life with beauty and an open heart. You will learn how to change your relationships from being sources of suffering and pain into gateways for infinite power and knowledge. This knowledge can result in a purposeful life filled with peace, understanding and relationships where you will explore yourself and fulfill your potential.

Relationships and the understanding of relationship are a lot of what life is all about. You will be amazed by its far-reaching implications. By reading and using the knowledge presented here I trust you will find, as I have, that relationships are about love, energy and *power*. Consciously using relationship will give you the ability to quit taking things personally and, when needed, turn your life on a dime in the right direction.

Whether you are Jewish, Christian, Muslim, Buddhist,

Hindu or from any other religious background, you can use relationship to become more powerful on the physical plane. The power of relationship encompasses every race and every creed and is at work on every continent for every person. If you pay attention to your relationships, you will have a constant and accurate barometer to navigate the waters of life. By using this power you will surf the waves instead of being pummeled by them. No matter what is going on around you, with a little practice when there are storms in your life, you will be able to use the power of relationship to stay at the eye of any storm.

By learning to work with the power of relationship you can even get a glimpse into how the universe works and *feel* and use the power of God that animates you. Now you might be saying to yourself, "I don't have a relationship with anyone special," or "I don't really have any friends." Well, *you have a relationship with life* and as long as you are living here on this planet that will continue to be true. The good news is that it doesn't take any special training, knowledge or ability to begin using this power! You can begin right now—wherever you are in your life.

With all that life has thrown at me, and the continual redefining of the person I am, I have maintained a loving relationship with my high school sweetheart for twenty-six years. In every area of my life I have made my share of mistakes and, despite this, I have survived and thrived through the rearing of three teenagers!

I have learned to face my challenges fully. I've allowed them to mold me into the man I could be in this world. This attitude has made it easier for me to do my best and to grow with every relationship I have had.

I started using this power more than twenty years ago when I made a decision to change my life. I made this decision to change my life in order *to save my life*. This is something we can all do. We can acknowledge that the way we live our lives right now, in this moment, is creating the rest of our day. We can own that the way we choose to live today is creating the string of tomorrows.

Once you accept this, you have begun the path, the path of releasing victimhood and becoming the powerful being of your birthright. You are then ready to embrace your relationship with life, whatever state it is in, and change it into one of *power* and meaning. You can embark on this journey as if your life depends on it. For, indeed, it does.

In this book I will take you through my voyage in life and tell you how I used this power to bring the peace and serenity that all of us are seeking. When you begin to use the *power of relationship* in your life you will laugh at the simplicity of it all. You will smile to yourself as you realize, "Of course, it makes perfect sense!" The strength that has eluded you for so long has been all around you, and right in front of your nose every step of the way.

Let's begin by defining power in this context. I am not speaking of control or power over others in any form. I am talking about the power, ability and strength to navigate life with *joy, beauty* and efficiency, the energy to accept wholly and with *grace* whatever challenges life brings and then consciously turn them into true gifts of power. When you recognize this power resides within you, you can use it to express yourself in this world as a magical being of the universe. You can step up and take the mantle of your birthright—where you will have the means to create a life that is, on purpose, fulfilling and even exceeding your potential.

I invite you to join me. Walk with me for a while as I share my knowledge about the power of relationship. Indeed, it is my honor and privilege to do so. I ask that as you do this you make a conscious effort to set aside the box you find yourself in, the box of your social conditioning and programming.

Introduction

Social conditioning and programming produce arguments in our minds about reality. Setting those aside can be done easily just by making a decision to be open as you read this book. As you open, the power of your spirit will work with you ringing the bell of truth. If you do this, you will be standing in your power, and you will naturally take what works for you and leave the rest. I wouldn't want it any other way.

Chapter One

Laying the Foundation
for Our Relationship

You and I have started our relationship, and it will be mutually beneficial if we both receive as much *power* as possible from our time together. To receive as much power as possible we must communicate effectively. Effective communication rests on a foundation of common understanding. We need to understand each other, and with this understanding you can obtain a *feel* for where I am coming from.

As you may have already guessed, the decision I made over twenty years ago was for sobriety. My life was a total mess, including my relationships. I decided to quit drinking and stop using drugs, and to do whatever it took to *live*. I didn't know at the time I had made a decision to change my relationship with life completely. One of the most important lessons or gifts of power this decision brought to me is since that moment I have entered into every challenge as if my life depended on it. Truly my life does depend on it, especially when I know this moment right *now* is involved in forming the rest of my life.

During those first years of sobriety I used what worked without really understanding how or why it worked. What worked and never failed me was to reach out to someone else whose path in life was similar to mine.

The first twenty-five years of my life may have produced a good deal of suffering but, thankfully, those years provided incredible gifts on which to build a life of love and meaning.

I was raised a Roman Catholic and had spent some time in my late teens and early twenties involved in mystical Christianity. As long as I can remember I have been interested in the "how" and the "why" of life as well as the power of the *One Spirit* many of us refer to as God. For instance, when I was young and I read about the miracles of Jesus, I wondered where those miracles were taking place now. Quite frankly, I wondered how these miracles could take place in my life, and why they weren't! I had many questions and very few answers.

From the time I made the decision to change my life and embrace sobriety my experiences have been remarkable, to say the least. I have had many trials and, yes, I have had a good deal of suffering. But the gratitude for surviving made room for me to accept life on life's terms and I rebuilt my life quickly.

I began what is often referred to as the spiritual path. I remembered all my questions as a little boy and set out to discover the answers. I would learn that *life is the path*, and it has all the answers I need. So simple! Everything I needed to move forward with clarity, power and connection was right there surrounding me.

I continued to do my best to turn all of my challenges in life into the great gifts they truly were. This meant that I must face and embrace my challenges fully no matter how difficult they were. I did my best to live in my relationship with God when one day, in one conversation, my entire life changed.

I was on the back porch of my home in Phoenix with a friend, and we began to discuss the influence of fear. We talked about how most of our fears never materialized and how all the worrying about the ones that did materialize never helped us handle them when they did arrive. We saw how we often created the things we didn't want by focusing on our fears. We chatted about how often fear is used against us when someone tries to manipulate us into how we vote, eat, what we buy, who we spend time with, and how we act or react in different situations.

Our list went on and on, and then it happened. I began to wonder out loud if we could live a life free of fear. We searched our experiences and neither one of us could come up with a reason why we couldn't do this. So we *made a decision!* My friend and I decided to embark on a journey together to see if we could completely eliminate fear from our lives. Life is fascinating and full of possibilities. Most of the time we really don't realize how one moment, one decision, can completely change its course.

Two weeks later, as a result of this conversation, I met a shaman. My intention upon meeting this shaman is important because it gives a glimpse into how *power flows into intention* surrounding service. This man had just moved into the area where I was living and I reached out to him, to help him.

Whenever we reach out to another in service we

become a channel for the power of the universe. We always benefit from this, beyond our rational minds' abilities to comprehend.

Before I continue with my story, let me clarify what I mean by fear. First, we have the survival instinct. As long as we are alive this will always be a part of us. Second, the fear I speak of is when my mind and ego take this survival instinct and run rampant with it. This leads right into stress, anxiety and obsessive worrying.

Since I made the decision to live a life free of fear I have met many people over the years that can't even imagine living a life without fear. Maybe it's not easy, but it can be done and it's really much simpler than you might think.

In trying to eliminate fear the problem lies in identification. Most of us identify with our bodies and egos instead of our true identities. When this happens to you, you have temporarily lost your conscious connection to the power of your spirit.

What you will find laid out in this book is a simple pathway back to the power of your authentic self. You will use the situations in your life to remove yourself from stress and anxiety by turning fear on its head and by using it to stay alert so that you are able to find out what is really going on with you.

Returning to my new friend, I continued to work on myself with him as a mentor. At first it was quite difficult for me to work with this shaman because of my programming. Consequently, our first order of business was to begin the process of removing my past and programming, or what is often referred to as social conditioning.

Our past and our programming are everything we have accepted, inherited or believed to be true based on what we have been taught, rather than what we have experienced. This includes our interpretations based on societal influences about what we have experienced, meaning we judge things as good or bad based on other people's opinions. As a result of this we can't really discern or *see* with clarity and receive meaning from many of the events in our lives.

Once I began to remove my past and my programming I began a yearlong process of finding out how most of the spiritual traditions have more commonality than they do differences. You and I will explore some of these commonalities in our time spent together. Perhaps someday the majority of humanity will engage in this exploration as well. Then we will have peace.

In the shamanic tradition I was initiated into, which is very similar to Toltec teaching, the shaman is someone who devotes his/her life to service. The shaman is in service to others, to the community and to him- or herself. We must not forget ourselves, for the great law of reciprocity states that we cannot give what we do not have. Reciprocity means an even flow and exchange of energy that implies being a vessel.

I was drawn to this new friend. I had this feeling deep down inside me that he had something I needed and wanted. I did not know what it was that he had, but this feeling gave me the courage to investigate beyond the limits I had with my current belief system. This investigation led to the realization that we are all connected to, and a part of, the same force many of us call God. Eventually a sense of wonder emerged about why so many of us argue and fight about the details of that relationship with God.

When I speak about *feeling* I'm not speaking about feeling connected to the fulfillment of bodily desires or feelings to satisfy the ego. For example, someone might feel good when he or she eats any kind of food without any consideration for his or her health. Some people feel better about themselves when they put other people down. In both of these examples the feeling is the result of massaging the ego or interaction with the physical body.

The type of feeling I will be referring to throughout this book comes from the expression of our intuition. This is often referred to as a gut feeling. When I met this new friend of mine it triggered my intuition, which produced a feeling of extreme attraction. I decided not to ignore this, and my life changed as a result. Our intuition is the expression of irrational knowledge that comes from our spirit. If we pay attention and learn to work with the feelings generated by intuition, then life eventually begins to make sense and take on a peaceful and exciting rhythm at the same time.

After studying with my new friend for about eight months, he felt I would be served best if I studied with his teacher. So my relationship with him shifted from his being a mentor to one of friendship and I entered into my formal training in shamanism with his teacher. As a result of this training I embarked on a path of developing my capacity as a healer.

Shamans and Medicine People refer to our path of training in life as the Medicine Way. It is interesting to me that so many different spiritual paths tending toward mystical are referred to as "the Way." We refer to the person who walks this path as the luminous warrior. The reference to warrior has very little to do with what most of us have tucked away in our programming surrounding this word. *The luminous warrior is a peaceful being who strives to live an empowered life, impeccably.* We define impeccability as the process of showing up fully in each moment and doing the absolute best we can. This is a simple definition, the application of which is profound beyond measure.

The luminous warrior knows the only way a person can truly know anything is through experience. So, when I speak of knowledge I am referring to the power you have received through your experiences in life instead of information you have gathered in one fashion or another.

Besides showing up fully in each moment, impeccably, the luminous warrior strives to live a conscious life that is centered in the heart. *Heart is synonymous with Christ Consciousness.* The luminous warrior is, therefore, a conscious person who is forever becoming more conscious of who he or she really is. Then the luminous warrior can become aware of his or her impact on everything and the ripples he or she leaves on the pond of life.

Typically I will refer to a conscious person instead of luminous warrior because it is a phrase more people are familiar with today. Please know that whenever I mention the phrase "conscious person" I am speaking of the luminous warrior, a being whose passion for life knows no bounds and who strives to shine with the Light of divinity, the true spirit of humanity.

Additionally, I have found that life is much more of what it can be potentially if I honor a particular experience and the way I *feel*. If an experience has brought a lot of pain and suffering with it, most of us are tempted to turn our backs on it and run from it in one fashion or another, even though we know that running away never really works. If we run away, we don't heal from the experience and embody the *power* from it. We create the same scenario again and again despite any efforts not to! Eventually we will have to face this same scenario, overcome it, and become empowered.

In honoring how I feel, I will refer to the One Spirit many refer to as God as the Great Spirit. This is an endearing term for me and I will use it throughout this book with the exception of the chapter on the *Unspeakable.*

While investigating different spiritual traditions I have really enjoyed uncovering universal truths. When a certain teaching is found within most of these traditions it is often referred to as a universal truth.

One of these universal truths relates to the real identity of each one of us. Each of us has an indwelling spirit or consciousness within the body. This spirit is the real you. Often it is referred to as the soul, consciousness or spirit. To date, modern science and medicine cannot determine what makes the body alive. They know a body lives, but they can't really say, "This is it. This is what enables the body to live." Isn't that fascinating? Often people say this another way: "We are spiritual beings having a human experience."

I will refer to your *real identity* as your spirit. Every tradition refers to your spirit, and the writings of these traditions indicate that your spirit is a *part of* the Great Spirit, not apart *from.* What a wonderful thought to consider! You are a *part of* the Great Spirit, not apart *from.*

In explaining one of the ways energy works we refer to the universal law of attraction. Very simply, this universal law states that like frequencies attract one another. When we change ourselves we attract different people and experiences into our lives.

One of the greatest gifts of this law is that it obliterates victimhood and the victim mentality. The friend with whom I set out to eliminate fear told me about something he had read, which I have never forgotten. "Every master knows that he or she has created everything in his or her own life, whether he or she is conscious of it or not." In my search through the different traditions I never came across any one of the masters who complained about his or her lot in life. This is one of the ways the universal law of attraction works; we are constantly attracting all of our experiences in life no matter what our perspectives are on these experiences. I have allowed this statement from my friend and the law of attraction to be a couple of my guiding principles. They have never failed me. If I am in a position where I am confused and wondering what is going on with my life, I open up. I open up my heart to my relationship with life. I take a look at what I am attracting into my life experience. I then find out why I am attracting this. With this knowledge I can eliminate it, if I want to, from my life experience.

Another aspect of ourselves is the human energy field. I call this the luminous energy field or energy field for short. On an energetic level this is the manifestation of the physical, emotional, mental and spiritual components of you. Within your luminous energy field are all aspects of you including all of your inherent potential as a child of the universe. Everything in your entire life, from your personality to how you will live and die, is contained within this field of energy. It is your own energetic blueprint. This makes perfect sense as science has taught us that energy informs matter, and that matter is really energy in a denser form.

So, there we have it. In this chapter we have laid the communication foundation for our time together. Let's begin an amazing journey into the *power of relationship*—simple and obvious in application, yet profound in scope. Wherever you are, you can begin to discover the magic of *being*, simply by using whatever is going on in your relationships and whatever is going on in your relationship with life at large. Let's start now. We have no time to waste!

Chapter Two

Obtaining the Relief You Need

When I made my decision to *live* and to do whatever was required, I became willing to go to any length to make change happen in my life. Consider how important this is. If you are ready to follow the spirit within you, the spirit who chose to manifest your life here on this physical plane, then you will own and accept whatever is not working in your life and you will do whatever is necessary to eliminate it.

Fortunately, we all have the perfect indicator on whether we are following our spirit or not. That indicator is *feeling*. Your spirit will always let you know if you are on the right track by feeling.

So here I was, only twenty-five years old, and I was at death's door with the knocker in my hand. Every area of my life was a complete mess and I felt beyond miserable. I was actually suicidal and completely depressed. In the hospital I had a flash of insight when I saw that I had created all my problems. This was the first time I acknowledged this to myself. No one could be blamed. No room was left for a victim mentality.

After this flash of insight I realized other people had reached this same level of despair, and in some cases even lower levels of despair. They had recovered from this point. I would seek them out, and if they would help me, then I would do whatever they told me to do to get better. With my life on the line, I would give a popular addiction recovery program my best effort.

Life really is a mystery of unimaginable proportions and impossible to comprehend with the mind. Years later I would learn that the easiest way to navigate this mystery is to pay attention, and let my feelings guide me.

An example of how I used my feelings to guide me is when I moved my family across the country to Arizona at the age of thirty-four. Both my wife and I had grown up in the Midwest and our entire lives were rooted there with a business, family on both sides, and three children in school.

As a family we began to take vacations to California, Arizona and Utah, and we fell in love with the West. My wife and I began to notice an intense feeling when we were on these vacations. The easiest way to describe this is to say that when we traveled West we felt as though we were coming home. When we did return home to the Midwest we became dissatisfied with where we lived. After our third trip in three years we returned to the Midwest with a feeling of mild depression.

We began to investigate these feelings and this led to contemplating a move. By working with these feelings we connected to our spirits trying to steer our lives in a new direction. This opened us up to the power necessary to have the courage to move, not only our family of five, but a business across the country to start a new stage in life. I say courage because we were moving to an area of the country where we had no support network of family and friends.

I have always marveled at how one moment can change the entire outcome of a person's life. I have no greater joy than participating in these moments, consciously, and in watching them happen for others. I wouldn't have manifested this moment *now* when I am writing this book for you if my wife and I hadn't paid attention to our feelings and moved to Arizona.

Now back to the age of twenty-five when I began my journey of freedom: My spirit knocked and I answered the call. I began listening to the counsel of other people who had obtained sobriety, and I acted upon it. I had become teachable.

One of the concepts these people taught me was that I really didn't know how to live. They explained to me that when life would challenge me, I would respond by taking it personally, or by blaming others, or by trying to force it to be different, or by insisting that life was not fair, or by…. The list goes on and on. I had absolutely no acceptance. I simply could not accept life on life's terms. All of this was ego and self-importance vacillating between self-pity and grandiosity.

What these more experienced people taught me (that's right, I hung out with the old-timers) is that, because I took everything personally, I was trapped within a narcissistic view of the world. From this skewed perspective everything revolved around me, and because I had no control over anything, I had a real problem on my hands! My self-centeredness distorted my thinking and eliminated my ability to reason. I could only succeed in trying to have some kind of a sane existence in between the land mines going off in my life.

This lack of control over life would build up within me until I had to escape. This is where an alcoholic is no different from most people. Without the emotional stability and maturity to accept the challenges coming my way, I escaped into alcohol and drugs. Other people may escape by avoiding a problem and running away from their challenges.

What these successful sober people taught me was I could not afford to let this buildup occur. Otherwise, I might end up going back to escaping, and if this would happen, I might never have a chance at sobriety again. Maybe this seems rather harsh but, remember, what we all know about life is that one decision, one moment, can turn the course of it.

So I asked these veterans, "What should I do? I don't want to miss my chance." I was told to take as many phone numbers as I could from anyone I felt comfortable talking with and who had at least two years of sobriety. I was then taught that whenever the buildup occurred I needed to reach out to my sponsor, who is like a personal mentor in the program, or to someone on my list of phone numbers. In theory this practice is simple enough, but the application of it can require a surprising amount of courage. A lot of people fall flat on their faces at this point. The key to making it past this point is holding fast to the realization that your old life has to change. In the Medicine Way we refer to this as death of the old. Death of the old leads to transformation. *Transformation is movement toward freedom.*

Refusing to engage others is stagnation on the foundation of self-importance. To clarify this point, let's look at a couple of examples. In our first example I have developed resentment against a co-worker and, after a few days of mental and emotional misery at work, I am finally ready to reach out to someone else to discuss this. As I am thinking about doing this, I have a thought: *You don't want to bother him with this little matter. Deal with it on your own.* This is the ego talking to me because it presupposes the person I contact will not receive any benefit from our exchange; my coworker deserves to have all of this nasty energy directed at him; and, last but not least, I am not important enough to be happy.

In our second example I am having trouble in my relationship with my wife, and I am bent out of shape about the way she is treating me. This has built up within me and is coloring my whole view of the world. As you can see, I am suffering. As I try to muster up the courage to talk to someone about it my mind tells me, *Wait a second! This is a private matter. You don't want to air your dirty laundry in public.* Again, this is ego as it assumes, at the very least, people are not very intelligent and they have no powers of observation; my wife and I are the only couple to have these types of challenges; my wife is wrong and doesn't deserve the benefits of getting along with me; and above all, I am right, and I want to continue being right, and I am unwilling to consider the possibility that I might not be!

Both of these examples have their roots firmly fixed in self-importance or ego. This ego will either make us feel "less than" or "better than" to separate us from everyone else involved. Definitely, this is not true. We are all individuations of the *One Spirit* and within the great mystery of life we are all equal. In the end this ego *nonsense* only has the effect of making us miserable.

Another common element of this warped viewpoint is where the whole universe revolves around "me" but I lack self-esteem. Most of us use self-importance to prop up or hide the fact that we have low self-esteem. This also makes no sense. It's a waste of energy, personal power, and it is an illusion. It is an illusion resulting from a limited, skewed perception. It doesn't take into account the universal truth that you are a spirit inhabiting a body. In other words, *you are identifying with your ego instead of your spirit.* This always leads to pain and suffering, which in one way or another, guides you back to your true identity.

How does pain and suffering guide you back to your true identity? Sooner or later you will grow tired of suffering and you will strike out looking for an answer. You will seek to find some meaning in your suffering. Eventually one of these quests will lead you to the realization that at some level you are creating all of your suffering. You will then ask why. When you ask this question you will realize that you are trapped in a limited perception of who you are. You are identifying with the mind and the ego. You will then ask, *If I am not my mind nor my ego, then who am I?* Once you ask this question, you are on the path to realizing your true identity: spirit. Eventually you might reach the point when you are ready to consider the possibility that your spirit is *One* with *The Spirit.*

At first reaching out to others to discuss my problems was not easy for me. Even though I had made a complete mess of my life and had become teachable, I still had a sizeable ego to contend with. Then the magic happened! I noticed something rather extraordinary occurred as soon as I started reaching out to others. After I had called or met a person to talk about the challenge, the challenge seemed either to disappear completely, or it lost its intensity. If my challenge only lessened in intensity, then I kept working on it. This always included speaking with someone about it. When I would overcome the challenge I could continue my path with a feeling of inner peace and the empowerment of having overcome that particular challenge.

I realized how much this did for the other person as well. Consider how you feel when you are able to help a fellow human being.

Something very powerful takes place during an exchange like this. Often the person I had reached out to had helped me change my perspective. The power of this should never be underestimated. If I had been trapped within self-importance, that person quickly pointed it out to me. (Thank you!)

Something else was taking place during these exchanges. I could feel it. I just didn't know what it was. This was the first application of non-attachment in my life. By some miracle that speaks volumes on the power of our spirit, I didn't care about not knowing why this worked so well and I let it go. Another way of putting this is that for once in my life I didn't need to know everything, and I didn't need to be in control. I knew reaching out worked for me, and that was enough. I had to save my life and get on with rebuilding it. It would be thirteen years before I would find out more about the underlying workings of these exchanges.

It had been a long wait but I would eventually have the next piece of the puzzle about why reaching out to another person is so powerful. The next step for me was to learn that we all have a luminous energy field, an energetic blueprint of ourselves. I was taught that everything about me is within this field of energy and that it attracts and manifests my life on all levels. I was shown how it is in constant motion based on the in- put it receives from the world around us and from us physically, emotionally, mentally and spiritually. Life was going to become a lot more interesting, make a lot more sense, and expose that it is infinite mystery all at once. Don't you just love it?

What I realized is that everything is energy, and that as we live here physically, we are all interacting on energetic levels as well. I became aware that I had been sensitive to this energy of interaction during my entire life. This awareness led to the realization that most people are also sensitive to this energy, albeit at different stages of development. I then began to *see* what was taking place on an energetic level with reaching out to others. The first thing I discovered was the energy of relief.

Let me use an example here to illustrate the energy of relief. We will use the workplace, a young man named Nick and his supervisor, Ellen. Nick's mother had passed away a few months ago and Nick had taken a couple of weeks off from work after her passing.

After Nick returned to work, his relationship with Ellen deteriorated. The relationship had now become a source of constant irritation and mental discomfort in and out of the workplace. A moment of change will soon manifest that will create one of those turns in life we have spoken about. Nick is at a fork in the road and he is going to make a decision to move in one direction or the other.

Ellen is a confident woman who knows what she wants in life and is not afraid to work to achieve it. These qualities elevated her to her current position as a supervisor. In the past Nick found her to be somewhat direct and perhaps at times a little stressed, but he attributed this to the pressures inherent in her position. Until now the only trouble and negative energy he had gotten himself into with this relationship was that of judgment. He accomplished this by telling himself that if he had Ellen's position, he would handle things differently. This perspective was the first sign of trouble, and we will address this in the next chapter on mirrors.

Let's first look at this interaction with Ellen from the perspective of Nick's energy field, and then we will get back to his decision about which way to move forward. Nick's relationship with Ellen is triggering several reactions inside him. These reactions result from his personal issues, and when activated, they produce clouds of dark gray energy in his energy field in an effort to be healed and released. These energies in Nick's field have become the lens through which he views and perceives his relationship with Ellen. They are affecting him physically, emotionally, mentally and spiritually.

Let's take a brief look on each level to see how Nick is being affected by these energies. We'll address the four major levels of his luminous energy field. Remember, this is by no means the entire picture when it comes to Nick's energy. I am detailing the energies so that you can get a feel for how every situation in our lives affects us on every level energetically.

On the physical level Nick is exhausted and irritable. Emotionally he is angry and resentful towards Ellen. Mentally he is obsessed with his challenges at work and he can't stop thinking about them. Spiritually he is forgetting that at some level he and Ellen are *One*, and that she is a human being who is doing the best she can, whatever that is. Nick has no acceptance, and he is in need of relief. Because of the energy building within his luminous energy field and via the universal law of attraction, his field is attracting more like frequencies to it. As a result of all this energy, Nick's perception has become distorted. He is viewing all women who are in their power through his lens of seeing Ellen. All of this energy is attracting more powerful women into his awareness and amplifying the whole situation.

This is the way energy works, and the way your spirit and the Great Spirit have set it up. They set it up this way so that you will address the situation, heal whatever it is, and immediately return to your true identity.

Most of us sense intuitively that we need to reach out to remove or dissipate this problematic energy. Other people are aware of this problematic energy as well. In this case Nick's co-workers are watching and wondering if Nick is going to explode. They can *feel* the energy as Nick and Ellen interact. Now, because of all the negative energy Nick has been projecting towards Ellen, she has changed. Ellen has become critical of Nick's job performance. This is obvious to everyone in the office, and most of them can see that Nick is getting a different Ellen than they get! Nick can go a long way toward leaving the victim mentality and its energy behind if he realizes that he is calling forth this behavior from Ellen. This isn't an easy task for most of us, but the rewards of doing so are almost magical.

Ellen is a person who is in her *power*. She shows up fully in each moment and does the best she can. This is the very essence of impeccability. Is she perfect? Most likely not, but she is living the path of the conscious person. Nick's work performance has suffered, and his performance needs to be addressed. This is in the best interest of everyone who works for the company. Ellen is aware of this energy with Nick and her changes in behavior towards him. She can *see* that Nick is suffering, and she knows all of this is happening for a reason. She doesn't know what that reason is, but she knows there is one.

As a conscious person Ellen knows it won't do Nick any good to coddle him and let him off the hook with his poor performance and attitude at work. She acknowledges that she has made mistakes as well, and that if there were do-overs, she would have done some things differently. Next time she will. Ellen will continue to show up fully in her *power*, present in the moment, and do the best she can with Nick. She also realizes that in the end, it is up to him. He can either work this out and heal whatever is going on, or he can manifest it again with other relationships. Such is the perspective of a conscious person. This is love that is unconditional. It would be much easier for Ellen to deal with Nick superficially and ignore the energy, or to use her *power* to remove it from the office.

Nick is in need of relief and he is going to reach out to someone in his life to dissipate the energy so that he doesn't blow up and dissipate it with an angry tirade. He is currently at a point that could wind up leading him in circles.

Lasting relief can only come from learning from challenges and by changing your own perspective. When a person does not obtain lasting relief, it often happens because most people reach out to someone whom they feel will confirm their points of view.

Nick could reach out to someone who would let him rant about Ellen and then agree with him that she is the problem. It is easy for us to imagine the outcome. Nick would receive temporary relief, but when again in Ellen's presence he would find that his discussion with his confidant only increased the charge he feels while he interacts with her. This happened because his friend only confirmed his view of the world, thereby strengthening the lens through which he had been viewing Ellen.

Let's look at another possible scenario that leads to permanent relief, objectivity and personal evolution. Nick has been spending more time with his Uncle Gregg since his mother passed on as a way to finish the grieving process and to reinforce family ties. He decides to bring up the situation with Ellen at work. His Uncle Gregg is a wise man with more life experience. Nick's mother was his sister, so he knew her very well. Gregg is also a kind man who has an ability to tell it as he sees it, with compassion.

Nick chose to speak to his uncle about the situation with Ellen. The perceptive reader will notice that Gregg didn't try to force his way into this situation. Nick's asking for help is an important part of the healing process.

Gregg is wise enough to know that Nick needs to get it all out and he needs *relief* first, before he can help him change his perception.

The easiest way to relate this part of the interaction is to switch to the dialogue of their conversation, which begins when Gregg asks, "When did you start having problems with your supervisor?"

"I always thought she was a little bossy but she really changed once I returned after Mom died," Nick said.

"Well, she is your boss. I'm sure it's a stressful position."

"I guess you're right," Nick replies.

Gregg sees Nick's sense of despair and makes a decision to steer the conversation in the direction of what he feels this is all about.

"Do you think this has anything to do with the death of your mother?" Gregg asked.

"What do you mean?"

"Well, what was your mother like?" Gregg looks away after this question to give Nick time to think.

"She always had my best interest at heart, but I always felt as though I didn't measure up," Nick responds.

"That's interesting. Do you think this is connected to your feelings regarding your supervisor, Ellen? I mean, she's a woman in a position of authority."

"I never thought of that."

Gregg gives Nick some more time to think and then responds, "Perhaps you haven't resolved everything surrounding your relationship with your mother yet. My sister was a good woman who did the best she could. She was a single parent who felt a lot of responsibility. I loved my sister, but I know as well as anyone that when she got stressed, she could be a handful."

"You're right about that," Nick replied and then smiled.

"Your mother may have pushed you hard but you turned out all right. You put yourself through college. You have a good job with a lot of opportunity. I'm sure this situation with Ellen will turn around."

"I never thought of it that way," Nick said.

Gregg senses Nick is at the point of surrender and decides to see if the time is right to help Nick change his perception.

"How has your performance at work been since you came back from your time off after the funeral?"

A long pause in the conversation occurred as the lights were beginning to come on for Nick.

"Well, it hasn't been up to the standard I normally hold for myself. So you think that Ellen's being on me about my work performance just reminded me of my relationship with Mom?"

"You said it. I didn't," Gregg responds.

Nick's work on his relationship with Ellen is by no means finished. By reaching out to another human being, he has changed his perspective about the whole situation. He now realizes that he views all women who are in their power through the lens he created as a result of his relationship with his mother. With this new perspective Nick remembers that Ellen's job is to make sure that she gets the best performance possible from all the employees she supervises. Nick can then have compassion and realize that Ellen's job is probably harder than it looks. He can now move out of being the victim and quit taking Ellen's behavior personally.

Not all of the issues contained in our energy fields can be tracked back to challenges surrounding the relationships with family members. I have used family situations with the examples in this book for a couple of reasons. First, I have found in my work that the challenges with our families are some of the first we address in clearing and becoming a conscious person. By addressing these unconscious patterns we learn to act instead of reacting. Second, by using patterns of behavior regarding our families of origin we are provided with clear examples that most of us can relate to.

It is impossible to put into words how much peace and power comes to us when we don't take things personally. Just as importantly, Nick can use his relationship with Ellen to release all of the unresolved emotions he has about his relationship with his mother.

An enormous amount of peace and serenity comes to us when we accept that most people do the best they can. Just like us, they are human beings, and we can accept that it is unrealistic to expect more from them than their best. This happens for us when we realize, and then adopt, the perspective that everyone's best is subject wholly to his or her programming and experience in life up to the present.

When I first became sober I had so many unresolved issues in my life that it was amazing I had time for anything else! All these issues resulted in my taking everything personally. This led to a lot of mental and emotional agitation that never allowed me to experience the peace and power of my spirit. I thank the Great Spirit that I had other people I could reach out to and thereby release the energy I was carrying around surrounding these issues. These wise people were not in my life to tell me what I wanted to hear. They were in my life to tell me what they *saw*, and to help me change my perception surrounding any situation so I could have peace and serenity.

Find a couple of people in your life to talk with when you need relief and guidance. Pick people whom you trust and with whom you feel comfortable. Please make sure you pick someone who is powerful and confident enough to tell you the truth as he or she sees it. Perhaps you can do the same for them. I am sure that you will then get the relief that you are seeking. No one needs to carry around unresolved issues and open wounds. Life is too short.

Chapter Three

Reading the Mirrors of Life

I continued to work with reaching out to others. Eventually I became one of the people others reached out to. This brought an enormous amount of gratitude. Any of you who have had the opportunity of consistently helping other people know what amazing energy this brings into your life. I felt I had discovered one of this world's best-kept secrets. In reality, I had. I just wasn't aware of the magnitude of what I had discovered.

In a short time my experiences taught me that whenever I began to suffer I was trapped within the limitations of my own mind. My mind created a limited perception surrounding whatever was going on right then in my life. Reaching out to others dissipated the energy, creating an opening for me to accept help in changing my perspective. At the end of the day it was always about changing my perception.

Years later I would learn power is generated and being used when we use our perception. I would also learn that it takes personal power to shift our perception.

Your physical manifestation is in itself an expression of power—the expression of the intent of your higher self. When you perceive something you are using that power, and energy is flowing to and around what you are perceiving. Another way to put this is to say that the Light of your consciousness flows through you and illuminates what you are perceiving. If you use that energy to evolve your awareness about who you really are, then you become more empowered on the physical plane.

I looked around at our world and I saw that the majority of people were not using this power of reaching out to others in a way that obtained the results they were seeking. They might like to chatter about their problems, but very few were interested in realizing that their own issues and the resulting perspectives were what needed to be shifted. In looking within myself, I determined this syndrome was often due to a need to be right, and an absolute terror over life proving otherwise! As you may remember, by working in the Medicine Way, I found out this need to be right was due to my programming or social conditioning.

I didn't have any time to wonder why other people weren't using this great power of relationship. I knew how to use it, and I would do so, not only to maintain sobriety but to get on with rebuilding my life.

Over the next twelve to thirteen years my life improved in every area beyond what I had previously even dared to dream was possible. I embraced change and began the journey of becoming more of the man I knew I wanted to be in this world. I set out to quit wasting time and this precious gift of life I had been given and to get on with fulfilling my potential. Every time my feelings and their subsequent emotions let me know I was off track, I reached out to someone and got back on my path. I felt I had discovered one of the greatest secrets to life.

After thirteen years of hard, joyful, sometimes painful work on myself, I was ready for the path of the luminous warrior. I was ready to become a conscious person. An old adage states that when the student is ready the teacher appears. I've found this to be true. However, being both a student and a teacher, I can also say that as students we need to pay attention. Every day most of us blow right by several teachers and the opportunities they present for real growth. I'm talking about every person we come in contact with, the mirrors they present to us, and what these mirrors tell us about ourselves.

The easiest way to begin thinking about mirrors is to consider the universal law of attraction in conjunction with our awareness. You will remember from the first chapter that the universal law of attraction says: Like frequencies attract one another. This law of attraction is always at work in every aspect of our lives. What we are aware of and what we focus on is no exception.

As I am writing this I'm thinking of communicating to you. I'm sitting on my front porch and the wind is blowing at varying speeds. The trees and plants are waving in this breeze. A jet is overhead, the birds are singing, cars are going by on the road nearby, and I can just barely hear the noise of vehicles on the highway off in the distance. The sun is coming up over the building across from mine, the gate is rattling in the wind and my coffee is getting cold.

With all these things going on around me I'm focused on my communication with you. At any one moment in our lives we're subjected to thousands of bits of information on several different levels. Consider that we have five senses, our intuition, and other extrasensory perceptions working all at once and at all times. With all of these stimuli in every moment, what determines where we place our focus? Because like frequencies attract one another, it's the universal law of attraction and the intent of our higher selves that determine where we put our awareness. Remembering this is key to working with the power of mirrors.

At this point it's helpful to provide an example of what I'm referring to and detail how a conscious person would use mirrors in his or her everyday life. Remember that the Medicine Way is a way to walk through life consciously. Walking in this way is often referred to as a path with a heart. Again, I've used an example of a pattern that has to do with family. Please remember not all of our issues, such as patterns, are the results from interactions with our families. Many times we incarnate with these issues and our families reflect them to us.

Bob has trouble getting to sleep due to some pressures at work over an important presentation coming up. After a night of tossing and turning, he awakens with a start as he has overslept. He has to hurry and get ready so he can make it to work on time. The suit he wants to wear that day is not in his closet, so he enlists the help of his wife, Sue, to ascertain its location. He's in a hurry and only focused on making it to work on time. Sue responds with impatience and a general overall attitude and energy that men are helpless. Sue has issues of her own, as she's getting three children ready for school. Bob is immediately angry.

The universe, and everything in it, is a mirror. The light of your own consciousness is constantly projecting itself onto the mirror that is the universe. The universe then reflects your exact position, which includes the *space* you are in, back to you.

Due to his stress and the energy dynamic with his

wife, Bob failed to notice from the several windows he passed in his house that it was a beautiful spring day. Not noticing this was another clue that something was amiss. Spring is Bob's favorite season of the year, and when he's in the space of a conscious person he almost always relishes the energy of springtime, and gives thanks, no matter how busy he is.

Sue lets Bob know that his favorite suit is in the downstairs hall closet where she always leaves his dry cleaning. He responds by snapping at her, and indicating that it would be nice, if just once, she brought the dry cleaning upstairs to their closet. Sue is aware of Bob's stress level, and despite his stress, she remains calm as she busies herself with getting the children ready. She's not going to play this game. So without emotional charge she informs Bob that if this is a big problem, he's always free to take and pick up the dry cleaning on his own. Sue does not engage Bob's energy, and so her response does not add anything to his agitation. Because his wife was detached with her proposal, he's left to face his anger and stresses on his own. After hurriedly kissing his wife and children goodbye, Bob jumps in the car to make the dash to work.

The next mirror Bob encounters is traffic. That's right, traffic! It's important to know how to determine if something is a mirror, or just a simple observation. The key to making this determination is the charge surrounding the encounter. When Bob's wife responded with impatience he was offended by her behavior and immediately got angry. He responded with many negative thoughts about her impatience, and an overall attitude that she was against him. So, without a doubt it was a mirror.

Now, as he sits at the first stoplight before getting onto the freeway, he's wrapped up pretty tight. The person in front of him is slow to respond to the green light and Bob blurts out with extreme frustration as he waves his arms, "Come on already, the light is green!"

Bob has had some training in how to live differently. As a conscious person, he cannot hide any longer from the way he feels. His actions and this latest outburst have left him thinking, so much so that at the next light Bob is the one who doesn't notice the light has changed! He comes to when the man in the car behind him lays on his horn and gives him a show of "affection" that involves using one of his fingers. Bob has had enough. He takes responsibility for drawing the mirror behind him into his morning experience and the use of his middle finger to make his point. Bob knows he has the power to change the course of his day and he's not going to waste any more time in getting to it.

As soon as he gets on the freeway and it's safe to do so, Bob phones his wife. Now Bob may sound like an oaf but in reality he's an intelligent man and has some experience in marriage. He decides to reach out to his wife, as an apology is in order! Bob has more than a few years under his belt with this type of endeavor, and when Sue answers the phone he begins the conversation with his apology. Sue gladly accepts his apology, and they begin the business of reading the mirrors. Bob goes on to relate the story of his recent experience with his fellow commuters.

You'll notice that Bob has determined to change his energy, and he's taking the first step by reaching out to someone. In this case it's his wife. Sue lets Bob know that she's aware he has been under a lot of stress lately with the upcoming presentation at work. She then proceeds to ask Bob how his relationship with his fellow employee, David, has been going. David is another mirror in Bob's life. David and Bob have been working together on this project and have had trouble coming to consensus on how best to get the job done.

We'll cover probing the *unknown* later but for the sake of clarity we need to touch on it here. By reaching out to someone Bob is searching the unknown.

Bob's impatience at home and at work has been growing. Today just happens to be the day when it reached a boiling point. Sue is a conscious person as well, and she has been waiting patiently for Bob to reach out so he can get on with the business of finding out what's really going on with him. It's no coincidence that all of this is coming to a head on the day Bob has to deliver his presentation.

With regard to his reaching out Bob has chosen well in reaching out to Sue for several reasons. First, she's not afraid to tell it as she sees it. Most of the reasons for this have to do with Sue being a conscious person. Sue is not afraid to tell Bob the truth, even if he doesn't want to hear it. Another reason why Bob has chosen well is that Sue is a woman. She is a physical representation and embodiment of the *unknown*.

A conscious person, whether male or female, can learn much about what's going on with him- or herself, and with this world, by watching the feminine mirrors as they appear day to day. The last reason why Sue is a good choice is that she's aware of the process she and Bob are engaged in. She knows that right now, in this moment, Bob is searching the unknown to find out what's really going on with him.

Back to our story: Sue is indeed a wise person, for

she knows that Bob's recent impatience with David at work is somehow connected to his stress and anxiety over this presentation. She also knows that Bob needs to figure this out for himself. All Sue has to do is ask a question so Bob will start searching the unknown within himself.

After letting Bob get everything out regarding his recent experiences at work Sue asks, "Do you think the energy surrounding your relationship with David at work is connected to this recent battle you have had with stress? I've seen you handle much more with way less anxiety." Boy, Sue is good! First she lets Bob finish dissipating the energy because she knows this must happen before he's ready to see something that is hidden about him. Then she ends with encouragement, which helps Bob have the courage to do what needs to be done. Bob realizes Sue is correct and lets her know this. He then gets off the phone, to put the time driving to good use.

Bob feels relief! For the first time today he notices how beautiful the morning really is. A wave of gratitude for his relationship with Sue comes over him. He feels better and he begins to contemplate. Contemplation is different than just reasoning as it involves the *heart* and *feeling*. Bob begins to work with the mirror that is

David. He notices the charge surrounding their relationship has mostly shown up for him as impatience. Bob asks himself, *What could this really be about?* He has always liked David and up until they worked together on this project, they had always had a smooth relationship. Bob continues to look into the mirror that is David to review some of the different times they have spent together. Then, out of nowhere, Bob has an uneasy feeling, and he realizes that David somehow reminds him of his father.

Bob then recalls exactly when his impatience showed up while working with David. It was during a specific conversation they had regarding the project they were working on. They had a difference of opinion on how to proceed with a certain topic, and David became outwardly impatient. For no apparent reason Bob gave in without making his point, and they moved on. From all outward appearances this exchange of ideas and energy seemed normal enough, but it wasn't for Bob. He now realizes that ever since this particular interaction, he has been holding resentment against David. Bob smiles as he continues to drive to work, and the pieces of the puzzle come together.

Bob now knows why the random thought came to him reminding him of his father. When Bob's father was trying to steer Bob in a particular direction he would use impatience as a means to get it done. Bob's father would also use impatience to manipulate people into taking action. He would use impatience with Bob to intimidate him and get him to take the action he wanted precisely when he wanted it to be taken. Bob, as is the case with many young men, has always had trouble speaking his truth with his father. That's why he didn't choose to work through David's impatience and make sure that David thoroughly understood his point. Bob now understands what he needs to heal within himself.

Bob also knows why he has drawn so many impatient people into his life recently via the universal law of attraction. It's because Bob himself is impatient! Bob now owns his impatience. He realizes that, just as his father taught him, he has been using impatience as a means of showing his disapproval of others. He's also been using his impatience trying to manipulate people into what he feels is the appropriate action. To accept this about himself is not easy, but Bob knows that accepting it will lead to more peace and empowerment in his life.

Right then, on the way to work, Bob gives himself permission to release this pattern of behavior, and makes a decision to engage with others without trying to manipulate them. He puts on relaxing music and begins to enjoy life again, even while driving to work. Bob appreciates the beauty of the spring day, and he suddenly notices how perfect all of this is. Spring is about new beginnings and new life. Bob is feeling life once again, and he's feeling a new beginning, both with this important presentation at work and the major realization he has had regarding his own behavior. He drives to work and arrives alert, relaxed and ready to do his best.

Bob will have to continue his work on fully eliminating impatience from his life. To do this he will have to pay attention and observe his behavior and feelings while keeping an eye out for using impatience to manipulate people. He will then have to choose not to engage in the energy of this behavior. The good news is that this will be so much easier for him to do because he's conscious of the pattern and he has used relief, mirrors and prayer to remove the energy of this pattern from his energy field.

Such is the life of a conscious person walking the Medicine Way. He knows that there's no knowledge as great as the knowledge of oneself. He engages with *all of life as a relationship* so he can get to know his greater nature, his true identity. To do this he must accept everything that is small about himself, and at the same time not accept it. He must do whatever is within his power to change the only person he can change—himself. One of the ways he does this with stunning accuracy is to work with the mirrors.

Now that we have covered an example of mirrors let's take a deeper look into what they really are. At any moment in our lives we have enormous amounts of stimuli. Obviously we cannot absorb everything that's going on around us at all times. To get by in life we have to focus. This narrowing of focus is achieved with the cooperation and guidance of our spirit. It can be helpful to think of yourself as a huge attractor field that's attracting every experience into your reality, including what you focus on. What you mirror and what you focus on shed light on the energy within you, and the energy within whomever or whatever is mirroring back to you.

Your spirit is always working with you, whether you are conscious of it or not. One of the ways your spirit works with you is through the mirrors. Your spirit is always guiding you into the realization that you are a part of All That Is. This is your true identity. Living in this power begins with knowing you are a part of the Great Spirit. This is a magnificent reality. Having just one experience of this will change you and your life forever.

For you to realize and live at this level, your spirit needs you to recognize every illusion that you accept about yourself as reality. These illusions you participate in attract people and situations into your life that you find uncomfortable. This is the emotional charge. This charge narrows your perception down to focusing in on these people and situations.

It's so easy to get off track if you blame others and put yourself in a victim position. The conscious person uses the mirrors to realize he or she is hiding something. If a person wants to eliminate the charge and quit attracting these people and situations into his or her life, then that person had better get on with finding out what the charge is all about. Thank the Great Spirit that this is not rocket science! The issues we are hiding from ourselves are usually directly related to any issues we find distasteful about a person or a situation.

For example, if you don't like dealing with angry people in your life, then search yourself and see what you are angry about. First ask yourself, *How are you projecting that anger towards others?* Next, go for dismantling it completely. This applies to actions that are physical and outward, as well as those issues that exist at the level of mind. Our thoughts are energy too.

Before we move on to the other types of mirrors let me say that the order is not in any way random. The reason I presented the previous type of mirror first is because it's the easiest for most of us to grasp and relate to.

You may be familiar with what has been presented so far on mirrors and refer to it as working with your shadow. To work with your shadow is empowering and is an essential part of getting to know yourself. Your shadow is any disowned or hidden aspect of yourself. Working with mirrors is one of the easiest and fastest ways to uncover and work with your shadow. By working with your shadow and getting to know it, you will be able to disengage from one of the games many people play—projecting their own darkness onto others so that they may get to know it.

Another kind of mirror that has to do with our shadow pertains to the greatness we see in others. Unfortunately it's just as common for us to disown our own greatness as it is for us to disown our own darkness. This is shadow as well.

In working with this type of mirror the charge surrounding the mirror is the key to identifying it as a mirror. However, this charge is different. It is a common occurrence for people to exalt another person and place that person above themselves, and everyone else. This is one of the ways we deny our own innate divinity. We have put this person on a pedestal and our own greatness is being mirrored back to us. We have denied this aspect of ourselves, so we need someone and the universe to mirror this to us. The good news is that we could not identify this greatness in someone else if it did not exist within us! Remember, you are looking in a mirror, and keeping this in the forefront of your mind is vital for unlocking the power of mirrors. Take a moment now to ponder humanity's response to all of the masters who have visited our planet.

Usually this type of mirroring will go on as long as necessary, until we're ready for the next stage of this slumber-filled scenario. Eventually we realize that this person is human. Masters are like us with the possible exception that they have developed congruence between who they think they are and who they *truly are*. Usually a person responds to this mirror in the way humanity has done for millennia. People criticize, engage in character assassination— they plot against and then they nail the person to a cross! Not a pretty scenario, to say the least.

This happens at this level of consciousness because the only way to deal with putting someone on a pedestal is to knock the master off as opposed to joining him or her. Every master knows this scenario must take place for people to realize that, just like them, he or she is human. At the root of this whole exchange people are uncomfortable with being human whereas the master celebrates it and thereby fulfills his or her innate divine potential.

So, how do we work with this type of mirror? When you have put someone above yourself outwardly or inwardly, begin by owning to yourself that you have done this. Then, list all the things you so admire about this person. Go through this list and try to perceive how you hide these great attributes from yourself.

Next, ask yourself, *How do I put this person above me? How do I deny these excellent parts of myself? Why do I hide my greatness from myself?*

Then work on combing your shadow. What this means is to examine the parts of you that you hide from yourself by asking yourself some tough questions. *Why do I deny these parts of myself? Why am I afraid to shine? What do I receive or create with this behavior?*

The masters weren't afraid to shine, and somewhere within you is a master in waiting. If this were not so, you wouldn't even be able to appreciate a master like Jesus, Mother Mary, Buddha or Krishna. This also applies to all of the amazing people here right now, writing and teaching about consciousness. They intend to share all they have realized with you.

We deny the higher self, our true self, for a multitude of reasons. They all come back to fear and ego. Once we have identified and owned this type of mirror, it's time to get to work.

Thoroughly go through your own personal history and see where you received the messages and the wounding that it's not all right for you to manifest your greatness. Ask the Great Spirit and your guardian angels to help you identify these reasons and release them. Go ahead. You won't regret it, and the world will be a better place because you did.

I've already mentioned that the universe is a mirror. Our internal condition is always mirrored back to us by what we create in our lives. This is what comes to us from the universal mirror.

I'm going to give an example of contemplation and the universal mirror. This story details how I work with the mirrors that are of the animal and plant kingdoms as well as the shadow element that is about denying our own divinity.

One of my favorite times of the year in the Southwest is the monsoon season during the mid to late summer. It is a time of intense storms including rain, high winds and lightning. Nature is a fascinating mirror. It mirrors beauty, perfect balance, abundance, timing and, of course, death of the old and transformation. It's difficult to deny that there's a power greater than ourselves when we stand in awe of nature's perfection.

One hot summer afternoon I was sitting on my back porch watching a storm roll in. Spider lightning lit the sky in the distance and was moving closer. This is the type of lightning that never seems to touch the ground. It weaves its way across the sky like a spider's web. Because this type of lightning never strikes with its power it reminds me that when there's true power, the need to use it rarely ever shows up.

The sun was still shining in my location, but the storm was only about eight miles away. It was large enough to cover the entire area of desert where I live. I looked at the giant saguaro cacti and recalled how they can drink up to ten gallons of water in a minute. A feeling of anticipation hung in the air, and the giant cacti reminded me of how important it is to recognize and take advantage of an opportunity when it arrives.

The whole time I was watching the storm a little bird was perched on a limb of a tree in my backyard. I began to watch it, and soon it had my full attention. The storm was now less than two miles away, and the winds began. Sometimes in these storms the winds can become quite destructive. The branch the bird was sitting on began to move in the wind, gently at first, but within minutes, the branch was bobbing up and down and flailing about. The bird continued to hang onto the branch.

So I said, "Little bird, you had better watch out."

"Why is that?" the bird responded.

"The wind spirits have arrived, and they're blowing hard. Are you not afraid that you'll be blown off your perch?"

There was a short pause in our conversation for a crack of lightning and the winds began to blow with even more ferocity. This little bird just hung on and at this point appeared to be a part of the tree's branch. Imagine that!

"Why should I be afraid of being blown off my perch?" the bird responded. "If it happens, I can always fly!"

I believe as long as I live I will never forget this moment. It was the moment when a little bird mirrored to me that I have the ability to fly. Since that day whenever I have been perched somewhere in my life and a storm arrives, as they sometimes do, I remember that each storm brings transformation. Then I remind myself that, like the little bird, I can always fly. The funny thing is since I've learned to work with relationship and mirrors I haven't needed as many storms to blow me off my perch. My intuition has guided me to fly off to new territory before any storms begin. If I become fearful about change, I remember that I can fly or get swept up by the storm. The choice is mine.

59

Now that we've become familiar with mirrors, we need to bring in an important element in categorizing them: time. Three time frames are associated with what the mirror is about for you: past, present and future. By working with the mirrors and bringing in time, you increase your ability to focus on what you are really seeing in the mirrors. This adds much power to the equation.

Let's look at a mirror that has to do with the past. You have come across a few people in your life lately who are less than truthful. Rather than being in a place of acceptance and realizing that some people just don't feel powerful enough to tell the truth, this is really aggravating to you. You know that you used to lie whenever it suited you, but you don't do this anymore. Why are you manifesting all these untruthful people in your life now? Your frustration increases until it threatens to take over your awareness. Of course, this ensures that you're going to do something about it. You decide to pay attention to everything the mirrors are telling you in order to solve this riddle. You intend to find your answer by looking into the great mirror that is your life in its entirety, from moment to moment.

Then one day, as you are working with these mirrors, what seems to be a random conversation with your daughter takes an interesting turn. She's talking about how she has decided not to spend any more time with someone she has been friends with for quite a while. This is a mirror for your daughter, but that's not your concern at this point. As your daughter begins to discuss how she feels guilty about ending this relationship, you become instantly agitated. Soon you also become overwhelmed with a feeling of guilt. This makes absolutely no sense, but such is the search that involves using intuition and the subsequent arrival of irrational knowledge!

You now have another mirror to deal with, and you decide that some contemplation is in order. Remember, contemplation involves intuition and "thinking with the heart." It is about allowing the mind to follow the heart instead of asking the heart to do as the mind reasons it should. As you contemplate the *feeling* of guilt you just experienced while listening to your daughter's story, out of nowhere you begin to think about the last person who lied to you. You wonder if perhaps there's some connection here. At this point you could reach out to someone to help you work through how these two items are connected, but in this example we're going to get to the point.

You then realize there are several lies you have told

in the past that have really hurt people. This is one of the reasons you made a decision to change and be a person who tells the truth. This is why the *feeling* of guilt showed up so strongly for you when your daughter was discussing her guilt surrounding ending the relationship with her friend.

You instantly realize that you need to release all of your guilt. You then rid yourself of its energy with the power of intention and a prayer.* As you continue to use intention and prayer over the next several days to release the guilt, something rather interesting happens. You become aware of a few areas in your life where you're still being less than truthful. You're surprised to find that you still have some remnants of being a liar left to deal with! This is amazing for you because even though you have done your best to be ruthlessly honest with yourself, you couldn't *see* these areas that still needed to be mopped up. This is almost always the case with a mirror that has to do with the past. That mirror is in our lives so that we can rid ourselves fully of the last few threads of an old behavior.

---

* *I give myself permission to release all guilt and shame surrounding everything, in particular* [insert circumstance here] *and I ask my guardian angels to help me release it, and I ask the Great Spirit to take it and dispose of it as It sees fit. Thank You.*

We've already dealt extensively with mirrors that have to do with the present. Now we'll move on to mirrors that have to do with the future. When I think of mirrors that have to do with the future I think of my story about the bird and the storm. By working with future mirrors I can fly off before the storm begins. A future mirror will let me know about behavior that has not yet manifested. I can stop it at the very beginning before it causes any problems in my life. *You* can stop something at its very beginning in *your* life!

One of the common ways a mirror shows up about your future is through the energy of judgment—judgments of others, and judgments about yourself. Of course, the key to identifying that it's a mirror is the charge of emotion surrounding the interaction with you and the other person. Remember, this charge can be completely internal. A charge is also how we determine if we're in judgment or using the power of discrimination. Judgment is an action that's thoroughly grounded in self-importance. We simply cannot see any situation for what it truly is when we're using judgment to elevate ourselves over someone else or to beat ourselves down.

Discrimination is a word in our language that has a lot of energy surrounding it. I am not referring to the action of judging a person or discriminating against them based on their religion or race. The power of discrimination is something completely different. It's using our God-given ability to choose between what's right and what's wrong for us. When we are using the power of discrimination we can separate a person from his or her actions.

Take a few moments now to ponder how much pain and suffering you have caused for yourself and others through the energy of judgment.

Now take a few moments to contemplate a few of your past experiences where you saved yourself from heartache by using the power of discrimination.

Doing this little exercise will lead you into *feeling* the difference between judgment and discrimination. Going forward and using this exercise surrounding judgments that come up can guide you through all of the judgments and into the power of discrimination, and ultimately into discernment. Discernment is the ability to perceive the difference between *Reality* and illusion.

Regarding judgments let's say you have a mirror in your life since you notice a huge charge surrounding a friend's behavior. The humor in this situation is that despite having known this friend for quite some time you never noticed this behavior before, and it certainly never bothered you.

You go through the process of looking at your own behavior and you can't find any area in your life where you're exhibiting this behavior. You then reach out to someone else to get another perspective. After experiencing the relief of reaching out, and with the help of the mirror you reached out to, you realize you are standing in judgment of this person, rather than using the power of discrimination regarding the behavior. You are then able to separate the person from the behavior.

You release all of your judgments surrounding your friend and the charge dissipates. Now you're capable of really observing your own behavior, and you come to the conclusion that this mirror must have to do with the future. In being completely honest with yourself you see that just recently a few behaviors resembling those of your friend have just started to seep into your life. They're so subtle that you wouldn't have noticed them without the help of your friend, the mirror. You then set out to eliminate the beginnings of these behaviors. You start by being grateful for your friend who is mirroring them to you. You dig into examining yourself and you determine what it is that you can learn if you move fully into any one of these behaviors. You take the lesson without taking the lumps!

Now let's consider future mirrors that have to do with denying your own greatness or potential. This almost always involves standing in judgment of yourself and making yourself feel less than someone else. You must look hard at yourself and see why you deny your potential. What is it that you gain from denying your own greatness? Are you trying to manifest a good quality through the negativity of judging yourself? Has your ego looped around on you and tried to convince you that you were being humble?

These are some of the questions that can lead you to discover why this type of mirror has arrived in your life. Through the process of soul searching we can bring to Light all the parts within us that need healing. This is a process that takes time, but if we are vigilant, the results will manifest into the emergence of a being who shines in this world as a true creator. That being is you!

Working with future mirrors is part of a shamanic technique that is often referred to as healing something before it's born. Take a moment to imagine how much more evolved the human race would be if we only repeated half the mistakes of the previous generation!

If you're at a point in your life where you're ready to work with future mirrors, then congratulations are in order. You are moving into a time of accelerated personal evolution, for you will become like the little bird who has the power to fly ahead of the storm, and still learn from it.

Before we go into navigating the *unknown* in the next chapter, let's look at one more example of a mirror. Let's say that you have been drawing people who really like to complain into your life. You know this is a mirror because an emotional charge surrounds their behaviors. You have searched yourself and your behavior and you're unable to identify any complaining about your lot in life.

In this case the mirror has to do with your identity. You're using another person who is complaining to define yourself as someone who flows with life and doesn't choose to whine about your circumstances. Another way of putting this is that you are bouncing off someone else to define who you are and the way you operate in this world.

Once you have identified that these people are mirrors whom you use to define yourself, you have a realization about where the charge for you is coming from. Going backwards and reviewing your behavior, you now realize that when you reached out to others to receive relief you began to complain about the complainers!

I mention this mirror last because we don't want to skip the process of ruthless self-examination. Self-examination takes courage and it's often human nature to do otherwise. If we don't want to admit to ourselves that we are behaving just like the mirrors in our lives, and we know about using mirrors to define our identity, then we can be tempted to call off the search through our own behavior. Next we jump to conclusions and assume this is only a mirror we're using to define ourselves. This will never lead to lasting results.

I have a practice I use to determine with accuracy which kind of mirror we are dealing with. If I immediately rush to defend myself, then I know that the mirror under examination most likely has to do with current behavior. So if I feel my walls going up and the words coming out very quickly saying, "I don't do that," I know I must continue searching myself and my life to uncover how I am doing what is being mirrored to me. Identifying this kind of defense mechanism quickly can be invaluable in achieving success with your search through the mirrors.

After years of practicing the technique of relief and learning to shift my perspective, I began working consciously with mirrors. It meant I would have to be thoroughly honest with myself. To live the life of a conscious person I would have to question both what's comfortable and what's uncomfortable. It meant accepting full responsibility for my life and leaving my victim mentality behind in its entirety. This is much easier said than done. At times I struggled immensely. I pushed forward through my struggles, because I could feel that this practice was going to be amazingly powerful. I had no idea how powerful.

The mirrors I no longer needed left my life. The people who were in my life to stay, changed as I changed, without my doing anything other than healing myself. As you can *see*, I no longer needed to call forth from them the negative behavior that had lived within me. Today, occasionally, I do call forth this type of mirror. When I do, I do my best to fly in front of the storm.

I continued working with mirrors for several years before the next aspect surrounding relationship showed up. This was a time of extreme gratitude. During this time I learned about the real meaning of *power*. Through relief and mirrors I began to *feel* I had discovered the great keys to love, peace and joy in life that so many strive for. I was ready for the next piece to the puzzle about navigating the great gift of life.

Chapter Four

Navigating the UNKNOWN

To appreciate the power inherent within relationship more fully let's look at life from a different perspective. For the sake of clarity I'm going to use a perspective from the Medicine Way that's easy to understand and assimilate. It is ancient wisdom handed down to me through the Q'ero lineage of Peru and closely aligned with Toltec teachings.

Because we are dealing with ancient wisdom you will undoubtedly relate to what I'm saying no matter what spiritual tradition you're associated with. Most of the religions or spiritual traditions have a common root in our innate desire to know ourselves. If you have no tradition, this is even better. When you have no tradition through which you have learned to view life, maybe you don't have a limiting view of the world regarding what's presented.

I had been using the gift of receiving relief for many years. I began working with mirrors in my relationships and this brought remarkable awareness into my life. After working with mirrors for a while I became cognizant of something else. I realized that for quite some time my challenges in life had become easier to handle. Upon contemplating this I realized what was happening. I was navigating the *unknown*. Because I was first receiving relief and then using the mirrors, I was navigating with ever-increasing efficiency.

Navigating and working with the unknown is a subject about which volumes have been written. For our purposes we will keep it simple and stay within the context of relationship.

Relationship and relationships are divine in origin and integral parts of the human experience. Think of an artist and the relationship an artist has with his or her creation.

The Creator has a relationship with its creation, and creation has a relationship with the Creator! You also have a relationship with the Creator and its creation.

This is true whether you're aware of this relationship or not. You *know* this to be true because you're interacting with the Earth, which is a part of creation. So, as you can see, we are all in relationship.

In the Medicine Way we divide the grand creation we are parts of into three categories: the *known*, the *unknown* and the *unknowable*. The implications of these divisions are extremely vast, but the good news is that we can start knowing about them right now, right where we are.

At this point we can glean from what we've already experienced and we can use it. To experience our next point, let's look at where you are in physicality right now. As you sit reading this book there is the known. For you the known is what you know and what you are aware of in this moment now. The unknown is everything that is not known to you. We will discuss the unknowable in a later chapter.

Please remember our discussion in the first chapter

surrounding the difference between information and knowledge. Knowledge is synonymous with power and it comes to us through experiences on the physical plane.

Perception is our first consideration in working with the known and the unknown. Let's assume you are sitting in a room while you are reading this book. If you pause to look around the room, at yourself and the other contents of the room, as far as your perception is concerned in this moment now, all that you perceive in this room represents the known.

Now let us consider another room in the place where you are currently reading this book. This other room represents the known and the unknown simultaneously. You may know all of the contents of the other room because you're intimately familiar with them through your experiences. However, as far as your perception is concerned it's the unknown, because you're not in that other room now so your perception can assemble the room.

To consider that our perception of something assembles that thing is a deep point indeed. Yet it's important enough to consider within our context. Let's take the example of the other room that you know but that's outside the scope of your awareness in this moment. Someone could have gone into that room and completely rearranged it without your knowledge. This might be highly unlikely, but it could still be true. This is how the other room is the known and unknown simultaneously. It's the known because you've experienced the other room and it's the unknown because your perception is not there now to assemble it.

How many times have you made a move in your life based on a decision about something you assumed was *known*, and it didn't work out for you as anticipated? Interesting point to ponder, isn't it? How many times have you had a challenge in your life and no matter how many different tactics you took, you just didn't move beyond the challenge?

Your answers to these dilemmas lie in navigating the unknown. If you knew the answer to whatever problem was causing your suffering, you wouldn't be suffering anymore. The problem is like the other room. We so often think we know the answer and when we set out to navigate the unknown we're only looking for information that confirms we're right! The need to be right comes from the ego. Most of the time this results in passing right by the solution to the challenge.

When we navigate the unknown we have to use the power of humility. This is true whether we're trying to find a solution to a challenge in our lives or whether we're trying to access different levels of being. Humility, like so many qualities, is not what we think it is. It is, among other things, realizing our *true nature* and its relationship to all of life. It's realizing that currently we don't *know* the answer we're seeking and we're humble enough to own this. The irony is that this is all so powerful because it insures that when we navigate the unknown in our lives we don't look to be right or assume we know where we're going beforehand. This leaves us open to all possibilities. By working with the *power* of humility we can move our lives from the probable into the possible.

When I have a challenge in my life I need to find out what it is that I am trying to learn from it. I then intend to find out how to overcome it and remove it from my life. I do this knowing that both things are currently unknown to me. I can do this with confidence and humility because I know that if the answers were known to me, I would already have the power and experience from the challenge. I wouldn't need it to be in my life in the first place! I know from my experiences that when it comes to accessing the unknown I must use the power of humility. Because of this I have an underlying confidence that sooner or later I will prevail. Because of humility this confidence does not turn into incapacitating arrogance. As a bonus, the solution often comes faster than anticipated.

No discussion of the known and the unknown would be complete without a little dialogue on the masculine and the feminine. Volumes can be written on this subject as well. What I'll endeavor to do here is to keep this as simple and as obvious as possible within the context of relationship and navigating the unknown.

If we want to know more about the complementary opposites that are the masculine and the feminine, we can learn more about them than is written in a hundred books by contemplating a man and a woman making love. It's a very simplistic approach—profound in its implications and easy and fun for most of us to do!

A man's sexual organs are visible. (They are located on the outside of his body.) Men tend to be very linear and rational in their approaches to life and in problem-solving. With this in mind we can say that the masculine is the known. Come to a man with a problem and he will launch into action in the direction he determines is correct in order to solve the problem. Launching into action is often to the dismay of the feminine being in his life because she really wanted him just to listen! Masculine energy is the energy of intention and action. This energy of intention and action is based on the known.

A woman's sexual organs are hidden. (They are on the inside of her body.) She is an embodiment of the unknown. Her approach to life is completely different than the male's approach. With the woman being an embodiment and in touch with the unknown, she's usually more comfortable using *feeling* to navigate the physical plane as opposed to using the rational mind. This ability to navigate using feeling results in the feminine ability to be in touch with and to keep track of what seem to be a thousand and one unrelated bits of information, much to the amazement of the man in her life. Her power is highly magnetic and lies in receiving the known and bringing forth new life, which is exactly what we do with each other in relationship. We navigate the unknown to increase our knowledge (the known) and use it as power on the physical plane.

We all have a feminine principle and a masculine principle, and this is true whether we are male or female. We all have the ability to use the known to get in touch with the unknown and thereby get to know ourselves more fully. We can then manifest our potential abilities as divine beings.

Another way of putting this is that we all have the potential of using the rational mind—the known—to make decisions exploring our feelings—the unknown—and then navigate the unknown in search of whatever solution we are seeking. Remember, we must not presume to know the answers beforehand.

One final point with the masculine and feminine that is incredibly beautiful and helpful in any relationship between a man and a woman, whether they are friends or lovers or both, is that when we have a relationship with someone of the opposite sex we're getting to know our *unknown* counterpart. The woman is getting to know her own masculine side and the man is getting to know his own feminine side. What an amazing journey life is!

Now let's pull this all together regarding the masculine and the feminine within the context of navigating the unknown to learn from our challenges. I *feel* that an example will work best at this point. I am intentionally using a woman and a man to take us deeper into the feminine and the masculine.

I have a client named Alice who has sought my help in resolving some issues at work. She has been having trouble with the toxicity of the work environment and her reactions to people at the office. Despite being a female, Alice is using masculine energy right now. She is in action mode to enlist the help of someone else to navigate this challenge. Alice lays out the challenge to me by describing the different interactions that have taken place at work. At this point I'm feminine, because I'm listening and receiving. I'm feminine relative to Alice because she's the one in action. Every time I ask a question to help her navigate the unknown or clarify a point, we're switching.

Alice also does her best to inform me objectively about the little nuances surrounding her workplace in general and she presents everything that comes to her.

She does this because we are navigating the unknown and at this point we don't know the solution. If Alice knew how to move beyond this, it would be known to her and she would have done it already.

Alice is intentionally using me as a mirror. To navigate the unknown she has pulled that mirror up close and personal so she can look into it with clarity and precision.

When navigating the unknown most likely whatever Alice decides to tell me is somehow related to the problem and the solution, even if it seems irrelevant. This happens because awareness and the energy of the problem inform us as she dissipates it using the process of relief. As Alice dissipates the energy of the situation at work by speaking to me about it, the energy will inform and direct the conversation. Therefore, anything she and I bring up is somehow connected even if it appears not to be.

The work environment, which contains so much toxicity, is also a mirror for Alice. Even though several people are involved and those people make up an entity that is a company, it's still a mirror.

The way that we know this is a mirror is because of Alice's charge surrounding the work environment. If this were not so, she wouldn't be irritated by her fellow employees' behaviors and, most likely, they wouldn't be toxic around her. Her work environment is mirroring something to her and because she's a conscious person, she knows this. Because she cannot read what's in the mirror Alice enlists my help—another mirror—to navigate the unknown, first, to read the work mirror and, second, to use the power received to change.

As a conscious person she knows that once she changes, her experience at work will change as well. She won't experience such a charge surrounding her co-workers' behaviors and those behaviors might stop altogether. This is a manifestation of true power as the conscious person knows that all he or she has to do is change him- or herself and the whole world changes!

After I listen to Alice and allow her to dissipate the energy she's relieved. We're now ready to read the mirrors and navigate the unknown. I start by asking Alice what actions she has been taking to deal with the situation. She tells me she has been doing her morning meditation and her energetic protection. Alice continues to explain that she feels great when she arrives at work, but as soon as the gossiping and backstabbing start, she feels completely drained of peace. I then ask her, "What happens next?" She tells me that she feels a complete drain of energy and it's not long before she begins engaging in these toxic behaviors with her fellow employees.

For the sake of clarity let's discuss Alice's history briefly. Alice is a powerful woman with a commanding presence. In working with the mirrors and her shadow in the past she realized that she would use her power in a negative way to put people down. She has acknowledged this behavior to herself and has realized that she did this because she was insecure. Alice has healed her own insecurity and is with me now to search the unknown with courage and an open heart. She is trying to determine whether her spirit is trying to tell her to change jobs or if there are still some energies within her energy field that need to be removed. Alice wants to know if she is attracting this behavior from her fellow employees because of something she is not seeing about herself.

I then ask Alice to contemplate if there are any other relationships where the old behavior is still evident. She spends a few minutes to search and eventually responds, "None that I am aware of." Notice how this answer is filled with the power of humility. Alice doesn't answer the question without pausing to search, and she is doing her best to be ruthlessly honest with herself in this search before answering.

A conversation between conscious people with the intention of healing and navigating the unknown is an act of unconditional love. It's both beautiful and powerful at the same time. If the people involved keep their heart centers open and stay focused on the task at hand, they will eventually prevail and make the unknown known. This might take some time, but it will happen if they hold the intention in this way. Once you have become comfortable doing this process, you can actually *see* and *feel* the Light coming in.

In this conversation the lights came on for both Alice and me at the same time when I said, "Perhaps this is your opportunity to choose differently and show the universe what type of work atmosphere you really want."

"What do you mean?" she asked.

"Well, we know that you have removed these patterns from yourself. Now the universe is asking you to show that in the physical."

"Yes, I realize this, but it's very hard now to choose differently while this toxic energy is so thick at work. How do you suggest I do this?" Alice asked.

I'm going to shift to the shamanic perspective for a moment and discuss energetic protection. You have the right to protect your own energetic space. This is the same as if someone tries to harm you physically. You have the right to defend yourself. In the case of Alice and her workplace all of this negative emotional energy is attracting even darker, more serious types of negativity. When I say darker, more serious types of negativity I'm referring to energies that seek to make life difficult on the physical plane. Almost every religion on the planet refers to these energies. Whether these negative energies are illusion or not depends on one's level of perception. I've found that in duality they're a force to be aware of and that we can eliminate them through the power of prayer.

Alice and I discovered she was responding to these more serious types of negativity. This resulted in her being tricked into thinking that this situation was only about her falling back into old destructive behavior. This, by no means, excuses Alice from participating in the toxic environment, and she knows this.

Alice and I then worked out a plan of action for changing the energy at work with the intention of protecting her luminous energy field. I asked Alice a couple more questions about her co-workers. Her answers revealed that they're really nice people. She has spent time with many of them outside of work and she reports they don't act the same as they do at work.

Alice leaves our session with a plan to ask her spirit helpers to change the energy while she is at the office. Again, she has the right to do this to protect her own energetic field. In addition to this she uses her power to remove all the negative emotional energy that has collected in the workplace while she's in it. She does this by using the power of her intention. From this point forward when there is a toxic buildup of negative emotional energy she'll use the power of her mind to visualize all this energy going into a black hole in space.

Alice has made a transition into using her power appropriately in the face of negativity. Instead of being a part of or adding to the problem, Alice is now in service with her innate power and is a part of the solution.

Alice called me again about a month later to follow up. She was very excited and reported that the energy in the entire office had shifted. Alice told me that everyone had calmed down and they were treating each other with respect. She mentioned how people were behaving more as they had when she would see them outside of work. Alice thought it was miraculous how everyone in the office had changed their behaviors.

Alice and I came together to navigate the unknown and we both ended up learning how negative emotional energy can hang out in a space and trigger the worst in people, despite their inclinations to do otherwise. We developed an action plan for this scenario that we have both been able to share with other people since then. Alice was able to begin using her power in a positive fashion, and her co-workers received the blessings of a better working environment.

Conscious relationship is truly an immense power that all of us can use to navigate life and the unknown that so often accompanies it. Remember one of the great keys to navigating the unknown and to receiving the answers we seek is the power of humility.

We must admit first that we don't have the answers we are seeking. We're not looking to have our view of the world confirmed. We must release the need to be right. Otherwise, we never even enter the unknown to navigate it in the first place!

We must reach out to others in relationship with an open heart. If we do this, then we will discover the small things about ourselves that are creating our problems. We will be able to heal them by choosing differently. This will eventually lead us to a more consistent working realization that we're divine beings navigating the physical plane. Once this happens our lives will never be the same. We'll attract people and scenarios that mirror our divinity to us and the world will be a better place for all of us.

Chapter Five

Activating the Universe's Power

By the time I assembled the next piece of power surrounding relationship, relationship had already done so much for me. It had become completely natural for me to reach out to others whenever I needed to receive relief. I had learned to use mirrors with increasing efficiency and eventually began to develop skill at navigating the *unknown*. All of this brought me an enormous amount of gratitude, which resulted in the opening of my *heart*. I developed the courage to lead with the heart. I feel that this is the common destiny of all men and women—*to follow and listen to the heart*.

As I began teaching and guiding others in the Medicine

Way it attracted more relationship into my life, which in turn brought more love and gratitude. This became an ever-expanding circle like the ripples on a pond. It's difficult to express in words how humbled and thankful I was for this *power*.

By the time I received the next piece in the puzzle on the power of relationship I had enough experience as a luminous warrior to know that I was still missing some of the details surrounding its power in my life. I knew I was already using this particular aspect of the power of relationship. I just didn't *know* what it was. What an interesting *space* this was! I could feel that something very special was happening. I would watch the results unfold when this feeling would show up; yet, I couldn't identify what this power was.

I'm speaking about a phenomenon I noticed occurring while I was asking questions to probe the unknown. I would be working on a particular challenge for several days trying to unravel its energy and remove it from my life. To do this I had to be aware of just exactly what the challenge was and what kind of energy I was dealing with. After several days of working on the issue with little progress I would involve my mentor. As soon as I would get him on the phone the whole picture of what was really going on with me would come into focus. Often this would happen without his doing a thing other than being the mirror I needed. At first I thought it was just due to the power of mirrors.

It was amazing that on almost every occasion I would ask a question that would lead me in the right direction very early in the conversation. After days of struggle, as soon as I involved him it became almost easy. Now my mentor is indeed a powerful being and I knew that his being involved in my searching the unknown greatly aided me in obtaining my answer, but I sensed there was more to it than that.

I feel that mentorship is a relationship that all of us can benefit from, no matter how wise we are and no matter how far we have come on our journey of realization in this life. For many of us others are on the path ahead of us, or at the very least, on the path beside us.

We can benefit immensely from developing a mentor relationship. It is indeed a relationship of power. I feel it's even more critical for people who have found themselves in the position of teaching and guiding others. An enormous amount of responsibility is inherent with teaching others and having a mentor is a great way to make sure that we stay on track. Though the gifts from this type of relationship are many, for our purposes I'm going to focus on one from the perspective of the Medicine Way.

In the Medicine Way we have a practice called "not doing." This means consistently checking in on your own perception. We call it stalking perception. No matter how far the luminous warrior has come he or she is never so arrogant as to think that stalking his or her own perception is not necessary. We have our feelings to guide us. However, it can be of help beyond measure to have a mentor to check in with. When we need to go where angels fear to tread, a mentor can be of enormous help as we wade through so many feelings, emotions and energies associated with our own human experience.

When we're responsible for helping others, whether we're a teacher, writer, psychologist, psychotherapist, healer of any kind or health care professional, having a mentor can help us stalk our perception and stay on the center of our path. Staying on the center of our path is important when so much is at stake for so many.

Surrounding the power of relationship, I began to experiment with this phenomenon of increased efficiency in navigating the unknown by paying close attention to it when I reached out to other people in addition to my mentor. Almost every time the same result happened. I would have my answer shortly after I involved another human being. My intuition told me that something very mystical and powerful was taking place, and that even with all I had done, I was now becoming ready to find out just how powerful relationship is.

Whenever we shine the Light of our consciousness on something we are doing, it increases in power, or if something is hidden from us, it comes to the Light. Indeed, we are amazing beings, all of us. So I formed an intention of finding out why this was happening, and just exactly what was happening. Then one day when I was on a walk and I wasn't expecting it, it came.

"For where two or three are gathered together in my name, there am I in the midst of them." I was taking a walk in nature when this scripture came into my mind. I feel that Christ Consciousness is our true identity; it is the Light of awareness. In that moment I realized that when I reached out to someone we were engaging the Christ within ourselves. This was why the process of navigating the unknown was so efficient. This made perfect sense and I was instantly filled with the Light of awareness.

When we consider Christ Consciousness and its relevant implications involving the *power* of relationship, we need to examine to whom Jesus was referring when he said, *"There am I in the midst of them."* Jesus is the Christ, so, when he said, *"am I,"* he meant that the Christ was in the midst of them.

We need to look at the meaning of *"in my name"* also. According to the Lamsa translation of the Aramaic text, the phrase *in my name* means "in his method, his religion, his approach to God." So from this we can conclude that Jesus said, "When two or three are gathered in the way I approach God, then the Christ I am is in the midst of them."

Now keeping in mind that every time Jesus referred to himself he was speaking of the Christ. From *Beyond Belief: The Secret Gospel of Thomas* Jesus revealed to Thomas, *"Whoever drinks from my mouth will become as I am, and I myself will become that person, and the mysteries shall be revealed to him."* This is just incredible! The words attributed to the Master Jesus tell us that if we drink in his words, meaning to take them in and let them become part of us, we will become the Christ. Not only will we become the Christ. In addition, the *unknown* will be revealed to us as well.

Throughout the scriptures Jesus the Christ is referred

to as the *light of the world*. This makes perfect sense to those of us who are familiar with Toltec wisdom and the trinity in other traditions. We have the Father, the Mother and the Son. The Father is the Spirit, the Mother is the manifested universe, and the Son is the awareness of both. In other words, this *light of awareness* is the Christ and in this awareness we are all *One* and a part of God.

I already knew these things when I was on that walk that day, and that is why I had the sensation I had been hit with a bolt of lightning. When I reached out to someone else with the intention of getting to know my True Self, I was activating the Christ in myself and in the other person. This was why the mysteries of what had been unknown were being revealed to us so quickly. We were remembering and activating our *true identities* as the *light of awareness, as the Christ.*

I could detail this further but I feel that this will only lead us down a rabbit hole of words. What I have presented on the Christ is close to information that can be *known* but not told. By no means do I have any expectation that you will take what I have presented here and believe it without searching your own *heart*. I only ask that you keep an open *mind* and *heart* as you investigate this in a way that makes sense to you. What I have said can be found in any spiritual tradition that I am aware of. It is all there. We only have to look for it and have the ears to hear it.

After the previous experience I was humbled beyond measure. How is it that, after all I had done and been through, I could deserve such a blessing? I would remember that it had *no-thing* to do with deserving it and everything to do with my *real identity*.

On the shamanic path we discuss serving our experiences as opposed to asking our experiences to serve us. If I only serve this one experience the rest of my life, I will never be able to repay all that I have been given so graciously by the Great Spirit and its *relationship* with my spirit. Through the power of humility I offer all I have for this great gift—my life.

It would be quite a while before my next discovery surrounding relationship. I was so happy and awed that I felt no need to explore further. When I was ready it would present itself, and, when it did, I felt I had come full circle. I had discovered and was using the very reason for life itself. My thankfulness knew no bounds!

Chapter Six

Connecting with the *Unspeakable*

Now, we are going all the way back to the beginning of relationship. In fact, we will be going to its origin as far as we can understand it. The beginning or origin of relationship might well be beyond what we're going to discuss, but if it is, it is thoroughly hidden inside the *unknowable*. If you remember in the chapter on the *unknown* I said we would get to the unknowable later. Well, now is that time.

One of my teachers taught me that the unknowable could only be experienced. This teaching is like all teachings in that they don't become a part of us until we experience them for ourselves. You might wonder how you can experience the unknowable. You can only have an experience of the unknowable in the same way you can experience anything. You must have the experience in your own life. I am speaking about an experience of the *Spirit* or your *True Self*, your own divinity.

We all have relationships in our lives. These relationships are about getting to know the True Self. Your True Self and its infinite mystery is a part of the unknowable. Although we can try to talk about it, it can only be experienced through feeling.

I can describe the taste and texture of a ripe, juicy orange but once you taste one, you will see that my words were completely inadequate. You had to experience the orange for yourself. It is the same with the Spirit and the unknowable: the Reality just can't be put into words.

An ancient phrase of wisdom says: *As above so below.* This means our physical world is a reflection of what is often referred to as the upper world or heaven. Many lineages of mystical spiritual traditions say that the *One Spirit* many call God moved in the void and fashioned its creation so that it could get to know itself. No matter what our belief system is, we can realize this as truth because the one thing every being on this planet is doing is having an experience of *its* Self.

It's time for us to explore the beginning. First I'm going to present the Toltec teaching on the origin of relationship and then present several other creation stories that detail the same perception, albeit in different words. I'll do this merely to illustrate how many different cultures and religions have come to the same conclusion.

With so much similarity between these views on cosmology, we can probably safely assume that the similarities are correct perceptions. You will have to decide for yourself, naturally. Pay attention to how you are feeling as everything is presented. This is important because it has been my experience that one needs to use feeling to grasp fully the power of relationship at this level. This subject matter is deep, but with a little patience and the power of feeling, it will all come together.

Let us first begin with the way Toltec wisdom lays out cosmology. This is my personal favorite because it's simple and because it has no religious affiliation. First we have the void; it is *no thing.* It's defined as the *Unspeakable.* It is unknowable. If we are honest with ourselves, we must admit that there's very little we know about the One Spirit many refer to as God. What little we do know about the void, from which all things come, has become known to us through our experiences.

Toltec wisdom tells us there was *no thing*, and then there was *some thing*. First was the void of no thing and then some thing stirred. It moved. This some thing that stirred and moved within the void was the *Intent* of the *Unspeakable*. We know very little about why this happened but we do know that, because something moved, the void could now be differentiated. When there was only the void, there was no thing. So, there was no way to know that it was there.

After this movement of Intent within the void of the Unspeakable, *Mind* came into existence as the Unspeakable became aware of its Self. Mind is the thinking, separating principle and it extended into manifestation, which eventually resulted in all of creation. For creation to begin, duality must exist (the Unspeakable and its Intent) and Mind (the separating principle) must know and have awareness. From this we can say that Intent and Mind form the awareness of the Unspeakable. It's aware of its Self.

From what we've discussed about the Toltec teachings on cosmology we can *see* that the Unspeakable has a relationship with its Intent and Mind, and that its

Intent and Mind have a relationship with the void. We can safely say that this relationship has something to do with the Unspeakable and Its awareness.

You have undoubtedly noticed that all of relationship is about getting to know oneself. We can see from the way Toltec wisdom lays out cosmology that relationship goes back to the beginning.

Now let's look at the way some other mystical traditions lay out the cosmos to ground our understanding further in such an esoteric concept. Another one of my favorite spiritual traditions is Taoism. Tao is pronounced "Dow." The following quotation is from the *Tao Te Ching,* authored by Lao Tzu. *The Tao gives birth to One. One gives birth to Two. Two gives birth to Three. Three gives birth to all things.*

Throughout the *Tao Te Ching* the Tao is referred to as the mother of all things. It is described as *unnameable* and *unknowable.* In several places Lao Tzu says that the Tao cannot be spoken about. It is the Unspeakable. Here Lao Tzu tells us that the Tao gave birth to the void. How do we know this to be true? Well, it's there and even though it's no thing, something created it.

The *One* that the Tao gave birth to is the void. The void gave birth to *Two* (the Intent of the Unspeakable). *Two* gave birth to *Three* (Mind). The void, Intent and Mind give birth to all things. These three combine for manifestation. This is, of course, a relationship—a relationship of the highest level at the very beginning before all things. It is interesting to note that this is a trinity. The trinity is found in most religions.

As you can see from this one small verse in the *Tao Te Ching*, it details a layout of cosmology almost identical to the Toltec teachings, and it details relationship between the forces of creation. The *Tao Te Ching* is peppered with similar references. I highly recommend getting a copy of this little book and reading it occasionally. It is a small manual of ancient wisdom. Its simple words give us a roadmap for peace regardless of what is going on in our lives.

Now let's look at what the Bible says about creation. *In the beginning God created the heaven and the earth. And the earth was without form, and void; and darkness was upon the face of the deep. And the Spirit of God moved upon the face of the waters. And God said, Let there be light: and there was light. And God saw the light, that it was good: and God divided the light from the darkness. And God called the light Day, and the darkness he called Night. And the evening and the morning were the first day.*

In this quotation on creation from the King James version of the Bible we have the same description of the beginning. First, we have "as above so below" because it says God created the heaven and the earth, and the earth was without form and *void*. We have the void and the darkness or *no thing* of the void. Then *the Spirit of God moved.* This is the Intent of the Unspeakable, God.

Then God says, "Let there be light!" This is Light of Divine Mind. God then separates the light from the darkness so that creation can happen. God names the day and the night. In the first chapter of the *Tao Te Ching* Lao Tzu tells us that naming is the origin of all things. For our purposes we can *see* that all these parts of God are in relationship. God is getting to know its Self through its creation!

This framework for trying to understand cosmology from Toltec wisdom, the *Tao Te Ching* and the Bible is almost identical to the Kabbalah, which is mystical Judaism. When God said, "Let there be light" this is the limitless light—*Ain Soph Aur* that is the Mind aspect of God before the physical manifestation of creation.

Let's use one more example from the *Rig Veda*, scriptures from the Hindu tradition. *In the beginning there was neither existence nor non-existence; there was no atmosphere, no sky, and no realm beyond the sky. What power was there? Where was that power? Who was that power? Was it finite or infinite? There was neither death nor immortality. There was nothing to distinguish night from day. There was no wind or breath. God alone breathed by his own energy. Other than God there was nothing. In the beginning darkness was swathed in darkness. All was liquid and formless. God was clothed in emptiness. Then fire arose within God; and in the fire arose love. This was the seed of the soul. Sages have found this seed within their hearts; they have discovered that it is the bond between existence and non-existence.*

Isn't it fascinating how similar these sacred writings are? It is the same teaching over and over again in slightly different language. In the *Rig Veda* we have the author doing his best trying to describe the void and it is helpful. Once again, as in the Bible, water is used to describe the void. This is to let us know that all life comes from this void. It is a way to relate to our experiences because we cannot have life without water.

I love the phrase, *God was clothed in emptiness,* because it helps us to understand the reason for creation. If only God existed, then how could God experience *its Self?* *Fire arose in God (Intent) and in that fire arose love.* This is why Toltec wisdom refers to Intent as being the feeling principle. This fire arising is also the birth of desire, the desire to create.

Now let's take a few minutes and use our imaginations to get in touch with the reasons why I have presented so many examples of *the beginning*. Imagine if there were no thing but you. Imagine there are no other people, no plant or mineral kingdom, no earth, not even a universe. There is just you and no thing else. There would be no way even for you to know yourself. There would be nothing to reflect the light that is you.

An all-encompassing fire would arise within you to know yourself. Well, this fire is within you and around you every minute of every day for your entire life. You are aware that you are alive or, more precisely, that you are *life*. You are this *Unspeakable* essence that is conscious of its Self.

If you took the time to work with your imagination in the previous exercise, then perhaps you got in touch with the void within you that stirs into an intense desire to create. This desire to create is love in action. It is the desire to know your Self through your creation.

In the Medicine Way we have many different techniques for realizing and working with this desire to create. The experiences as a result of these techniques remind us that we have plenty of time but none to waste. This demands that we fully embrace all that our essence brings into our experience. We realize that the "bad" as well as the "good" shapes us into who we are becoming. This results in a marvelous passion for life that is difficult to describe.

One day I was celebrating this passion for life with joy and gratitude. I began to contemplate all the people I know and how grateful I am for each presence in my life. I was filled with the power from all of my experiences, and then it happened. I remembered the reason why I had been so focused on using the power of relationship.

Every time I reached out to another to get to know myself, I was using the same level of *power* and the same *intention* that began creation in the first place.

Tears rolled down my face. How could I have been given such a gift? Certainly no thing I have done made me worthy. I had come full circle, and I understood why I kept exploring the *power* inherent in relationship. I knew now why I had decided to share fully what was in my heart, even when it was painful to do so. I could *see* and *feel* why we are all engaged in relationship in one form or another. At the core of my being I *knew* if I never gained another piece of knowledge, this would be more than enough.

You see, my dear friend, each and every *One* of us is engaged in using the same level of *power* and *intention* for creation itself every time we connect with the other. We reach out with the fire of desire to receive relief. When we do this to remove the little self so that we can know the *Self,* we activate the Christ within. With the power of the beginning and the awareness of the Christ we can read the mirrors, navigate the *unknown* and realize once again that we are a part of the *Unspeakable.*

Chapter Seven

My Dream for Us

An ineffable essence permeates you and surrounds you at all times. Perhaps you know what it is, or you have spent your whole life looking for it. The great irony is we can't find it because it has never been lost. It just *is* and always will *be* and *it is you*. All we have to do is remember it.

This essence cannot be spoken about but it can be heard in laughter and the song of every bird. This essence cannot be seen but you can bear witness to it in every act of the *heart*. It cannot be tasted and it cannot be smelled but you can *feel* it when you smell a flower and when you taste your favorite food. This essence cannot be touched, but you can feel and sense it when you caress your child or your beloved, or when your child or your beloved caresses you. This essence is *life* itself, and you are an important part of it. In my dream for us we will all remember to *feel* it.

Life is a mystery of grand proportions. Sometimes its awe-inspiring power brings us to our knees. In those moments we must take *heart* and remember that we are still a part of this all-encompassing presence that is life. Life is awareness itself—the awareness of the *Unspeakable*. All of your experiences will mold and guide you back to this realization, if you let them. In my dream for us, this realization will become commonplace.

To honor and participate fully in this great gift of life we have been given, we must reach out. We must reach out to the other—the other being another aspect of Great Spirit's creation, so that we can get to know ourselves and so the other may get to know its Self. When we engage in relationship consciously, we get the opportunity to release our burdens and use the power of perception without the influence of illusions created by fears from the ego.

Once you have removed the energy associated with your burden, you can look in the mirror and see your Self as it really is. Then you are ready to navigate the *unknown* and find out what is truly going on with you. Now you are in a position to change, to evolve into the person you are becoming. Because you are working with *power*, you will have the courage necessary to deal with yourself, heal and move into the Self.

You continue to work with all the mirrors in your life including the mirror that is the universe. When you reach out to the other at this stage you are activating the Christ in your Self and the other person. The unconditional love of the Christ returns to you. Once again you remember this is your *true nature*. This attracts different experiences into your life.

You continue to move forward in beauty and bliss. You are aware you are the *no thing* that is the Spirit. When there is *some thing* you get to work and start the whole process all over again. However, now you are *aware* that you are using the same level of power and intention used for creation in the first place. You realize that you are consciously participating in the evolution of awareness itself. You are involved in the Great Spirit, the Unspeakable, the One Spirit God becoming aware of its Self through its creation.

What more could we ask for?

In my dream for us we do not forget about the power in connecting with one another. With email, the

Internet and text messaging I feel it is so important to take the time to connect and honor the great gift of life and celebrate it with others. Our technology threatens to isolate us further as much as it has the possibility of keeping us connected across the planet. Pick up the phone—at least with this we have *sound*. When we meet face to face, we have *sound* and *light!*

I have seen so much miscommunication happen with letters, emails and faxes. Perception is very powerful, and we can forget how prone it is to projection because people see what they want to see. An email may produce a feeling, but is it the feeling its sender intended? This is especially dangerous as we all become more intuitive.

Does an email contain the light in someone's eyes or the sound in his or her voice? In my dream for us we will use technology, but cease to have it use us.

Our technology is a reflection of the dualistic nature of our existence here on Planet Earth. We have the Internet where we are all connected and at the same time separate. It can help us increase our knowledge and stay connected across the planet, or it can add to our sense of being disconnected. It is the same for us. We are all *One* and at the same time we are individuals. We can choose to experience ourselves as individuations of the

One Great Spirit, or we can live in the illusion of separation from other individuals and from the *One*.

We are all connected in a great web of life that is magnificent, to say the least. When this web of life is seen or felt, it leaves the person awestruck with silence at its sheer magnitude and brilliance. In my dream for all of us we will once again *realize* this great web of life and own that it would not be the same without each and every One of us. Then our world will collectively return to balance and reflect back to us the peace we have obtained within. In my dream for us we will collectively identify with the essence of *life*, instead of all the forms it has given rise to.

We have come a long way together, you and I. I want to say how honored I am to have shared this time in relationship with you. I thank you for giving me the opportunity to share my journey—from receiving relief to my realization of the *Unspeakable*.

May you realize that life is a feeling and that you're an expression of divinity. May you realize that you, personally, are a great gift to this world. My dream for you is for you to know, without a doubt, that none of this would be the same without you.

Namaste.

East – West Prayers

I have used the symbol above throughout this book to depict two points in our day, its beginning and end. This symbol simultaneously represents the sunrise and sunset over the ocean of life.

Every day each of us is presented with the opportunities that are embodied in the following prayers.

Morning Prayer — East

Great Spirit, Earth Mother, with the dawn of this new day I ask for your help to walk this day with the clarity and vision brought to me by the winds of the East. Help me to remember that I can use the power and wisdom from all days preceding this one without reliving them.

I am filled with gratitude for this new opportunity, and may I walk in beauty today, in balance with the great gift of life. May I honor the gift of this new day by living my potential and destiny within the great web of creation.

Evening Prayer — West

Great Spirit, Earth Mother, I thank you for another day. With the setting of the sun and the death of this day may I feel the gratitude for every moment it has brought me.

With the impeccability of the winds of the West help me to absorb every moment of this day's experiences without attachment. I honor this day by allowing it to die and transform me with its power.

Please help me to arise unencumbered, yet empowered by the past, for a new day tomorrow with clarity and vision.

About the Author

John English is the award-winning author of *The Shift: An Awakening*. He is a teacher, international speaker, visionary, entrepreneur, and shamanic healer who is deeply concerned with activating the power of the human spirit to dream a new positive future for humanity, individually and collectively.

John's soul purpose is to assist others in making a positive shift in their lives and to live in the power of their Spirit. To fulfill this mission, he teaches and writes about a variety of holistic subjects, including health, intuition, meditation, energy healing, stillness, shamanism, and the medicine wheel.

John is a family man with three children and has been married to his high school sweetheart for 26 years.

In addition to numerous national one-day workshops, John teaches the journey toward empowerment through Dreamtime's Medicine Wheel program, an immersion into the ancient wisdom from the Q'ero of Peru.

To learn more about John and his work visit his websites:

www.mydreamtimellc.com and
www.nospiritleftbehind.com.

Permissions